Sex
for One

Sex
for One
THE JOY OF
SELFLOVING

Betty Dodson

*Illustrations by
the Author*

Crown Trade Paperbacks/
New York

This book was previously published in different form under the titles *Selflove and Orgasm* and *Liberating Masturbation*.

Published by Crown Publishers, Inc., 201 East 50th Street, New York, New York 10022. Member of the Crown Publishing Group.

Crown Trade Paperback™ and colophon are trademarks of Crown Publishers, Inc.

Manufactured in the United States of America

Design by Beth Tondreau

Library of Congress Cataloging-in-Publication Data

Dodson, Betty.
  Sex for one.

  1. Masturbation.   I. Title.
HQ447.D59   1987   306.7'72   87-12039

ISBN 0-517-58832-3

10   9   8   7   6   5   4   3   2   1
First Paperback Edition

This book is dedicated to me.
Without my selflove it could
never have been written.

Contents

Acknowledgments

My gratitude goes to Grant Taylor for the indispensable part he has played in the creation of this book. For the past twenty-three years, we have had an ongoing passionate dialogue about the politics of masturbation. In 1970, I let him convince me that I could write. Since then, he's been a demanding teacher, a patient assistant, a testy devil's advocate, an expert editor, a first-rate word processor, and, always, my best erotic friend.

Also I want to gratefully acknowledge all the women and men who have shared their orgasms with me in my Bodysex Workshops. They have been my inspiration and my teachers. And to all the wonderful people who took the time to write, I say a thousand "thank yous" for all your love and support.

I'm also grateful to my agent, Frank Taylor, for believing in the book and finding the best publisher to do it. My appreciation goes to Esther Mitgang and Liz Sonneborn, my enthusiastic editors at Harmony Books.

CHAPTER ONE

Liberating Masturbation

Masturbation is a primary form of sexual expression. It's not just for kids or for those in-between lovers or for old people who end up alone. Masturbation is the ongoing love affair that each of us has with ourselves throughout our lifetime.

In the age of AIDS, you'd think we could at least celebrate masturbation as the safest sex. But making love alone is still society's dirty little secret.

It used to be said that incest was the last taboo, but that word is now used freely. Incest has even been dramatized on national television. So why hasn't there been a story about a preorgasmic woman who learns how to masturbate to orgasm and starts enjoying partnersex for the first time? Or think about the educational value of a script dealing with a premature ejaculator who teaches himself how to prolong erection with masturbation and turns into a fabulous lover. My retirement fantasy, if it ever got aired on prime time, could change the image of old age. There are thirteen of us old folks living together in a commune. Every full moon we gather in front of the TV set to watch a new pornographic video of politically incorrect sex. After brewing a strong pot of tea, we plug in our vibrators and settle down for an evening of orgasms. The rocking chairs creak, the vibrators hum, and occasionally one of us smiles and nods yes after a particularly good one.

Our cultural denial of masturbation sustains sexual repression. From childhood through adulthood, we feel guilt and shame over masturbation. Deprived of a sexual relationship with ourselves, we are easier to manipulate and more accepting of the status quo. I believe masturbation holds the key to reversing sexual repression, especially for women who think they're "frigid" or aren't sure whether they're having orgasms in partnersex. The same is true for men who are "premature ejaculators" or for those men who can't get enough stimulation to have an orgasm from intercourse.

Masturbation is a way for all of us to learn about sexual response. It's an opportunity for us to explore our bodies and minds for all those sexual secrets we've been taught to hide, even from ourselves. What better way to learn about pleasure and being sexually creative? We don't have to perform or meet anyone else's standards, to satisfy the needs of a partner, or to fear criticism or rejection for failure. Sexual skills are like any other skills; they're not magically inherited, they have to be learned.

Masturbation is our first natural sexual activity. It's the way we discover our erotic feelings, the way we learn to like our genitals and to build sexual self-esteem. It's the best way to gain sexual self-knowledge and to let go of old sexual fears and inhibitions. For women especially, it's a way to build confidence so we can communicate clearly with our lovers. When we're asked what feels good, we will have the courage to let go of our little white lie, "Oh, everything you do feels good."

At the end of the Sexy Sixties, during my erotic evolution, guilt-free adult masturbation became an important part of my sexual healing. As my sexlife went from zero to fantastic, I wanted to share the good news. At first I expressed my joy with erotic art. Next I started writing articles and speaking out about women's sexual liberation. At the time I thought women suffered more than men from sexual repression, and liberating masturbation was my feminist commitment. Soon masturbation became my field of expertise, mostly because no one else wanted to talk about it publicly.

When I began speaking about masturbation with the women in my consciousness-raising groups, I realized there was a need for CR groups devoted entirely to sex. My next step was running masturbation workshops, called Bodysex Groups, for feminists who were willing to take sexual love and liberation into their own hands. Then in 1974, *Ms.* magazine published my views on masturbation in an article. The reader response was so immense that I was inspired to publish a little book the same year titled *Liberating Masturbation; A Meditation on Selflove.* With the national recognition the book brought, I found myself with a full-time job that I kept trying to get out of. "I'm a fine artist, not just a jerk-off artist," I complained. But being committed to a concept was similar to having a child: it meant giving unconditional love, even on the days I hated being "The Mother of Masturbation."

Each year I resigned from teaching masturbation in my Bodysex Groups, and each year I set up another round of workshops. Being a sex teacher without any academic credentials was a bold move, but where could I go to get a degree in masturbation? I decided my fine-arts background qualified me to explore the aesthetics of sexual selflove. Some days I saw myself as a performing artist, and the workshops were simply my new art form. Other days, I saw myself tilting at windmills and was ready to disappear into my studio, never to be heard from again. But after fourteen years of this unique fieldwork, I've awarded myself a Ph.D. in masturbation.

I used to say masturbation leads to sex, but now I know masturbation *is* sex. The next time someone asks, "When was the first time you had sex?" the appropriate response would be your first memory of masturbation, not the first time you had partnersex.

Although I expected masturbation to be a household word and part of every high school's sex-ed program by the eighties, here I am, still liberating you-know-what. Friends sometimes ask why I keep hanging in with the subject, saying, "These days everybody knows that masturbation is okay." But the truth is that people still can't use the word freely or talk openly about the subject—particularly in relation to their own sexlives. It's true hardly anybody believes that masturbation causes insanity or warts anymore, but most of the current books and articles about sex, while deploring the frightening old myths about masturbation, still damn it with faint praise. Worst is the implication that masturbation is an okay substitute for "something better." Whenever I get a new sex book, I immediately look up "masturbation" to find out where the author really stands on sex.

Aside from its importance as a form of sexual self-help, the benefits of masturbation are many. Masturbation provides sexual satisfaction for people unable to find partners. It's a way for teenagers with irrepressible sex drives to have orgasms without the possibility of pregnancy. Masturbation also provides a sexual outlet for couples when they are separated, when one partner is ill, when one partner is not interested in sex, or when either partner cannot get enough stimulation to reach orgasm through sexual intercourse.

Masturbation can also be done with a partner (or partners) as a valid alternative to intercourse; sharing masturbation is an important addition to the sexual repertoire of couples. Masturbating prior to partnersex is a way for men to eliminate sexual urgency and rushing. It also provides safe sexual satisfaction during the last stages of pregnancy, and can give relief from menstrual cramps. Masturbating to orgasm is relaxing and helps induce sleep. Finally, and certainly a consideration these days, masturbation is the basic form of safesex.

It's important to remember that there are all kinds of people who are not in a relationship—some out of choice, some because they're waiting for the right person to come along, and some because they lack confidence or have a physical disability. Some women and men just out of long-term marriages find it too painful to reestablish themselves in a relationship, but they still feel sexual. And we often forget about the sexual needs of the elderly, especially a wife or husband widowed after fifty years of marriage. There are still others who have no choice but mastur-bation; they're in prisons, nursing homes, mental institutions, or the military. Acceptance of masturbation can make a lot of people's lives more fulfilling.

Another reason I keep hanging in, urging the whole world to say yes to sex in its most basic form, is to counter the voices of organized groups committed to condemning masturbation as "sin-ful." The Roman Catholic church heads this list. It also includes the fundamentalist Moral Minority, which still clings to the doctrine of sexual guilt from the Old Testament. (The biblical story of Onan spilling his silly seed isn't even about masturba-tion; it's about coitus interruptus.) Organized opposition to masturbation, like opposition to pornography, is actually oppo-sition to sexual arousal; to be turned on is somehow considered antisocial. In truth, it's just the reverse: to be sexually repressed is antisocial.

When I was a high-school student obsessed with sex, full of romantic myths, thinking my acne was from too much masturba-tion, and lacking any information about birth control, I was a potential victim at all times. What a difference it would have made if there had been a Professor of Sex at East High! My fantasy of her lecture goes like this: "Sex will change throughout your life. After hot, romantic sex, which is all you understand now, there will be the sweetness of early married sex, the mystical quality of procreative sex, and the comfort—or boredom—of long-term monogamous sex. Most of you will get divorced and have another phase of hot romantic sex, and run the cycle again. Those of you who are lesbian or gay will follow a similar pattern. A few of you might go on to explore sex in depth, getting beyond conventional sexroles and labels, and experiencing bisexual threesomes and groupsex. But take note! The most consistent sex will be your love affair with yourself. Masturbation will get you through childhood, puberty, romance, marriage, and divorce, and it will see you through old age."

I am renewing my commitment to validating masturbation as a primary form of sexual expression. *Sex for One* is an erotic concept whose time has come. Universal acceptance of masturbation is the next step in civilization's sexual evolution.

My futuristic fantasy for sexual liberation goes like this—it's New Year's Eve, 1999. All the television networks have agreed to let me produce "Orgasms Across America." Every TV screen will be showing high-tech, fine-art porn created by the best talent this country has to offer. At the stroke of midnight, the entire population will be masturbating to orgasm for World Peace.

Romantic
Images
of Sex

As a teenager the movies of the forties gave me delicious close-ups of long wet kisses, misty sad eyes, and thousands of "Darling, I love you's" along with tearful embraces after painful separations. Those were all images of romance. Hollywood did not supply images of sex. When it was time for actual sex, the scene always faded, and the camera zoomed in on a huge wave crashing against the rocks. I knew that was supposed to be the orgasm, and it made me long for passionate sex with my future "perfect lover." Some day we would get married and live happily ever after. It was the romantic ideal that all young girls shared, so I was quite normal, except for one thing: while I was waiting, I was secretly enjoying orgasms with myself.

My favorite teenage masturbation fantasy was "The Wedding Night." I pictured myself as a glamorous movie star: no fat, no acne, no braces on my teeth, and beautiful breasts instead of a flat chest. While my husband awaited me in bed, I disappeared into the bathroom to put on the latest fashion in nightgowns. My sexual buildup was imagining every detail of my perfect beauty. Orgasm came when I dropped the exquisite lace peignoir, offering my naked loveliness to my husband. I never visualized what he looked like, or what we did sexually! That fantasy was a combination of *True Romance* and *Vogue*—my romantic pornography.

Masturbation was my sexlife until I was twenty years old, when I finally "went all the way." My family, my friends, the world at large, and I pretended masturbation didn't exist, and, therefore, the pleasure I experienced was not real. My sexuality did not exist until I found true love in partnersex.

Nevertheless, masturbation has continued to be a part of my sexlife. I'm not typical in this respect. I've learned that many people don't masturbate regularly once they are past childhood exploration. Some people have no memory of any masturbation. A lot of women and men who do resort to masturbation do so with feelings of guilt or a sense of loneliness.

I am, however, typical in most other respects. I was subjected to the same barrage of sex-negative conditioning we all get. I was made to feel that I should get all of my sexual pleasure from my lover's penis, not from his hand or his mouth, and certainly not from my hand by myself. But the nontypical part of me refused to shape up. Even if masturbating was wrong, I kept on doing it. I now realize learning how to have orgasms from masturbating allowed me to enjoy partnersex.

Coming from the Bible Belt in Kansas, I knew very well where the church and conservative moralists stood. But when I moved to New York at age twenty, even my open-minded friends thought masturbation was a second-rate substitute for "the real thing." That was in the 1950s. My only source of sex information were marriage manuals and random bits of Freudian psychiatry. When I finally made it to the couch, my therapist and I had the same romantic image—mature sex was having vaginal orgasms from intercourse within a meaningful relationship. Adult masturbation was okay if I didn't do it too much; otherwise it would be compulsive or infantile behavior. I was sure that several times a week was too much, so with grim determination, I set out to find Prince Charming in order to live happily and orgasmically ever after.

Throughout my twenties, I had superromantic, monogamous love affairs with passionate orgasms from intercourse. My lovers and I always planned to get married, which justified the sex. Masturbating while I was involved with a man would have meant there was something terribly wrong with my sexlife. Each of these affairs lasted about two years, and the breakup was always devastating. Being romantically in love was like mainlining emotions. I was hooked on my beloved, and there was no way I could live without my fix. Never once did I become a smart romantic addict who had learned how to move along to the next lover without suffering. At the end of each affair, I nearly wiped myself out with sorrow, regret, despair, or rage.

After years of searching for love, my prince finally found me. It was a romantic dream come true, and at twenty-nine, I got married, just in time to escape the horrible fate of going over the hill alone. During the first year, I felt our sexual exchange was modest, but my therapist said we would be more passionate in bed after we made our "marital adjustments." I quit my job and concentrated on marriage. I was now economically secure, but I was getting more and more concerned about our sexlife.

In our marriage's second year, we were having sex about once a month. When we did make love, my husband would come too fast, and I wouldn't come at all. Afterwards, we'd both be embarrassed and silent. When he was asleep, I would quickly and quietly masturbate under the covers. I'd do it barely moving or breathing, feeling sick with frustration and guilt. Since we were in love, I couldn't understand why we weren't into sex.

I was a doomed romantic junkie, trapped in a marriage that wasn't living up to my romantic ideal. Sometimes I felt it was all my fault. Our lack of sex meant I wasn't holding up my end of the marital bargain. I had no sexual value, and he didn't really love me. Torn between blaming myself, blaming him, or blaming the institution of marriage, I was too busy to consider sexual alternatives. With joyful masturbation, I could have had an orgasm every day and one decent fuck a month. But no! Every time I wanted sex, I had to depend on my other half, and sometimes he really did have a headache.

Over the next few years, there was so much tension and so little communication in our marriage that I stopped wanting sex with my husband altogether. Instead, I began creating monumental masterpieces of art. But in the sixth year, no matter how much I tried to sublimate my desire, hot sexual memories crept back into my consciousness. Once my husband went on a business trip and my horniness spilled over into a private one-week orgy of drawing my sexual fantasies, getting turned on, and masturbating way beyond the point of going blind. I drew all the exciting sexual perversions I could think of, which were actually very few—oralsex, fucking doggie style, and a threesome. Overwhelmed with guilt at my hedonistic debauchery, I destroyed the drawings. I actually tore them up into tiny bits and flushed them down the toilet, afraid someone might find the scraps in the garbage and put the pieces together.

Of course my marriage fell apart. I wanted orgasmic partnersex to be part of my life. We had a civilized divorce, drawing up our own settlement, and I had enough money to make the transition into being single again. But after all that dependency, I was worried about reentering the job market and was filled with inhibitions about reactivating my sexlife. Though I projected the image of a sophisticated New Yorker, inside I felt more like a thirty-five-year-old virgin. So it was with a mixture of fear and excitement that I embarked upon my erotic journey.

It was 1965, right at the time American women were launching the second wave of feminism. Reading *The Feminine Mystique* by Betty Friedan made me an instant feminist. Shattered forever was the myth that Everywoman's complete fulfillment could be found in marriage. I no longer felt like a freak for wanting to be an artist instead of a wife and mother.

I began to understand how the politics of marriage had affected my sexuality. Although I said I married for love, I had really bestowed my gift of sex in exchange for economic security. Because I lived in a society that didn't give equal pay to women, I was unconsciously bargaining with sex for marriage—still the best financial deal for women. Whether I was saving sex for my prince, freely bestowing it on my lover, or granting exclusive rights in marriage, I was doing business with sex. When the female genitals have economic value instead of sexual value for women, marriage becomes a legal form of prostitution. It's no wonder that some wives feel like underpaid hookers and some husbands feel like overworked johns.

As long as I insisted on the romantic ideal, I was sexually repressed and economically dependent. Wanting to be taken care of meant pleasing men, so naturally I wanted the earth-moving Big O from fucking. He might not love me if I wanted to have my orgasm from masturbation or oralsex. Unable to enjoy sex as an equal, I ended up using it to possess my lover. Possessiveness caused sick feelings of jealousy that always led to violence. I justified this in the name of love. Terrible fights and arguments were called "lovers' quarrels." Instead of conforming to traditional ideas, I began to question the existence of a "perfect lover" or the desirability of having *every* orgasm from intercourse. And I questioned the validity of getting *all* my financial and emotional security from love and marriage.

Getting married is one of the most important decisions people make. Since marriage is the business of sharing sex, money, property, and the likelihood of raising children, it needs to be given the same dignity that making a million-dollar deal gets. Any good business person knows the importance of a contract to clarify terms and reach agreements before a legal partnership is formed. When I got married, I simply said, "I do."

The reality of traditional marriage and the romantic image

of sex are a stormy combination. Couples unwittingly play power games with unstated rules and unwritten agreements. In one game, the poor man is responsible for running the whole romantic fuck. Despite his own background of sexual repression and deprivation, he is expected to get an erection from her naked beauty, keep his erection, arouse her passions, and hold off his orgasm until she reaches hers. He's required to do all this without any information about what really turns her on. The woman is passive, beautiful, and graceful while she waits for this incredible experience called orgasm, and when nothing happens, she concentrates on the romance.

In another game the poor woman is responsible for the man's erection. She does oralsex to get him hard and remains focused exclusively on his pleasure. He gets on top and does what feels good for him, and she accommodates him, going into her act of passionate sounds to excite him all the more. He comes, she fakes it, and he dozes off holding her in his arms. She's happy because she has pleased him, and she loves the closeness. He's happy because her response has proved he's a good lover, and he loves her loving him.

According to Kinsey, on the national average there are only 2½ minutes of thrusting after penetration. That's not enough time for anybody to have much fun. As we limit sex to the duration of erection and penetration, we perpetuate the battle between the sexes. Most of the time it's in the missionary position, which satisfies the romantic stereotype of the passive woman and the dominant man. He tries to hold back while she struggles to come, and often they both fail.

There is a vast range of erotic delights available if we simply get more open-minded about what sexual pleasure is all about. When the only image of romantic sex is passionate orgasms from intercourse, it creates a ritualized genital fixation that leaves no room for play or growth. Once we let go of the idea that there's a "right" or "best" way to have sex, we'll all have love and orgasms in abundance.

16

CHAPTER THREE

*Erotic
Images
of Love*

M y first postmarital relationship was a sexual turning point. Blake was an exciting man. At the age of forty-two, with enough money to retire, he'd wrenched himself away from his workaholic ways as a professor and publisher to seek pleasure and peace of mind. Soon after his divorce, he quit therapy, came off the addictive pills prescribed by his doctor, and stopped drinking his ritual martinis before dinner. At the time we met, I'd been off alcohol for three years, so we were both completely drug free. We started mainlining sex.

We were both delighted with our intense, experimental love affair. Good sex quickly changed my image of ecstasy. In the past

I'd been grateful for one orgasm during lovemaking. What you don't know, you don't miss. Now I was having several orgasms, and their intensity actually alarmed me. After every big one, I needed reassurance from Blake. Did he think the neighbors could hear me? Was he sure that I wasn't damaging my body? Was it really okay with him when I carried on like that? It was my introduction to pleasure anxiety, the fear of having too much of a good thing. He told me I was the sexually responsive woman of his dreams.

It was a thrill to be able to talk honestly and openly about sex. Our exploratory conversations quickly got onto the subject of marriage, monogamy, and sexual repression. I told him about my guilt-ridden marital masturbation, and he told me about his. He talked about the "toning down" of sex that had evolved during his seventeen-year marriage. Lovemaking had become totally predictable, and the sexual constraints and lack of communication had also been depressing. He was sneaking extra orgasms by masturbating in the bathroom. Though he longed for sexual variety, he had agreed to be monogamous, and he was too idealistic to seek extramarital sex. His only alternative was masturbation, which would have been okay if he could have done it joyfully. But, like me, he'd felt sick with frustration and guilt. As his self-esteem was eroded by this process, he began to regard himself as a dirty old man.

Through our discussions, I began to understand how our whole antisexual social system represses us. We couldn't even touch our own bodies for sexual gratification without feeling sick or guilty. That realization made me so angry that I resolved to banish sexual guilt from my mind once and for all. It would no longer be part of my life. I intended to explore sex passionately and in depth without the interference of church or state. The best way to learn about sex and pleasure was to have a lover with an open mind. Blake and I quickly moved beyond traditional sexroles. With our healthy inquisitiveness, we both experimented with being receptive and assertive by being on the top or

bottom, and we took turns doing each other with oralsex and erotic "hand jobs."

It was a special meeting of minds as well as bodies when we got together. What a joy it was to find a man who agreed with me about sex! We started gathering bits of sex information that supported our ideas about the importance of masturbation. Masters and Johnson had just published their findings on female sexuality, which demolished Freud's idea of "mature vaginal orgasms." They found all orgasms centered in the clitoris, and that categorizing orgasms as clitoral or vaginal was incorrect.

The controversy of clitoral versus vaginal orgasm was not an issue for me because I was getting both kinds of stimulation at the same time. As I lay on my back, Blake would enter me from an angle while lying on his side. With his free hand, he delicately massaged my clitoris with moistened fingertips while we did a slow, sensuous fuck. It was the best of both worlds. During another one of our erotic interludes, he placed my hand on my clitoris, encouraging me to stimulate myself. Another sexual break-

through! Now we could both concentrate on our own sexual movements and sensations. I could control my buildup by slowing down or moving faster. We were having bigger and better orgasms, and sometimes we even came together, which was fun now that it wasn't a hard-and-fast rule. Pleasure was begetting pleasure. With all that wonderful sex, I was surprised to discover I was masturbating more, not less, whenever we weren't together.

We both knew that masturbation had saved our sexual sanity, and we vowed that we'd never again consider it a "second-rate" sexual activity. Although we'd decided that masturbation would be a natural part of our sexual exchange, actually sharing it for the first time was difficult for both of us. After all, masturbation had been a private activity our entire lives. Naturally this new kind of exposure made me feel very vulnerable. Once I made it clear that I wasn't dependent on him for my orgasm, I was confronting the possibility of upsetting *his* romantic image. I felt tentative about taking such a big risk with sexual honesty. At that point, any criticism from him would have sent me scurrying right back into the old missionary position.

22

First I decided I had to get up enough nerve to watch myself masturbate in front of a mirror alone. When I saw I didn't look funny or strange, but simply sexual and intense, I was amazed. Until that moment, I had no visual image of myself as a sexual being. With this new erotic information, I was able to make the breakthrough with Blake. We celebrated our Sexual Independence Day by showing each other that we could have first-rate orgasms by ourselves. We both loved it! Masturbating together demystified the romantic image of orgasm, and I stepped down from my pedestal to become a sexual equal.

New discoveries and insights came quickly with this freedom. Being able to masturbate together made all sorts of experimentation possible. From watching, he learned which patterns of manipulation and contact were the best for me. I learned what he liked by watching him. Without the interference of our own responses, we were able to observe each other carefully and in detail. We could see the total body involvement in sexual buildup and orgasmic release. It was a home-study program in Human Sexual Response.

Psychologically our intimacy deepened. There was an even greater freedom to be more honest about our feelings—perhaps a fuller recognition of each other's humanness brought about by the sharing of this basic sexual activity. There certainly was an increased feeling of comfort. For example, my sexual buildup to orgasm usually took nearly thirty minutes, and I would often get hung up worrying that he might be getting tired. Now that we knew I could continue by myself, the pressure was off both of us. I stopped trying to hurry up and come.

With the liberation of our masturbation, we no longer had to conform to each other's sexual needs. If one of us didn't feel like having sex, the other was free to masturbate, which often turned on the one who hadn't been in the mood. He was able to tell me there were times when he actually preferred to masturbate rather than to have intercourse or oralsex. He began to realize how much pressure he'd been under to perform sexually. It had

been nearly impossible for him to say "no, thank you" when sex was offered. The best way to avoid sex and save face was to start an argument. But now that he was more liberated, he was overcoming his socially conditioned fixation that fucking was the only "real" kind of sex.

Honest-to-goodness sharing was the essence of intimacy. We felt more at ease, and sex was a lot more fun. Becoming responsible for our own orgasms was a basic statement about individuality and equality. It established us as people who had a choice when it came to lovemaking. We were moving away from romantic sex toward the infinite delights of erotic loving.

Society has been slow to provide any positive images for divorced people, single parents, surviving partners, or older gay people who end up living alone. The idealized image of the young romantic couple whose love for each other mysteriously conquers all will get us through our twenties, but like Romeo and Juliet, it helps to die young. Getting married and staying together forever may work for some people; for millions of others it doesn't. There needs to be more support for the positive aspects of two people "getting apart." We should be congratulated. Divorce doesn't mean failure, and living alone doesn't necessarily mean loneliness. Two of the happiest days of my life were the day I got married and the day I got divorced.

Neither Blake nor I wanted to get married again, nor did we want to live together. We'd spent the first half of our lives immersed in "togetherness." Now we wanted to practice the art of "separateness." We wanted to find out who we were as individuals. It was a radical concept in 1966, and friends thought we were crazy. Why would lovers want to spend time apart? After a year of erotic loving, we set out to sow our erotic oats separately, convinced that sexual love was inclusive, not exclusive.

Learning how to live without owning another person went in stages. First Blake and I stopped going steady. We started dating other people and exchanged information about our successes and failures. We discovered the joy of sharing erotic love with each other and several other people at the same time. We no longer expected our sexual exchange to last "forever." Now we could simply enjoy it for as long as it was good.

Being a whole person took me back to that period in my childhood that I loved the best. It was just before everyone started going steady. We hung out in small groups, and the world seemed larger with more possibilities. But by high school, hanging out with friends on Saturday night became a memory because suddenly everyone traveled in twos, like Noah's ark.

Within five years Blake and I reached the critical point that comes in most relationships. The old sexual charge had diminished, and we wanted to have our primary sexual exchanges with other people. In a traditional relationship, we would have had to sacrifice sex for the security of staying together. In another five years, we would have been cheating on each other with clandestine affairs. However, our radical idea of separateness paid off. There was no love-hate drama, and I had no urge to destroy myself with despair or rage. We even double-dated with our new lovers and continued to be good friends.

All of my lovers had the potential for becoming friends, and all of my friends had the potential for becoming lovers. I went on to experiment with having roommates, living communally, and sharing vacations with my erotic friends all over the world. My security for old age was living more fully in the now. Better than blue-chip stocks was having selflove, good health, creative work, and a big erotic family of friends.

Blake and I have continued to be an important part of each other's lives, sharing a dynamic dialogue based on a mutual interest in sex. Our meaningful friendship goes on to this day. It's a different kind of love story.

CHAPTER FOUR

Sex Art

As a classically trained artist, I painted the nude. I thought of my art as sensual, never overtly sexual. My art had always remained on the periphery of sex. But the first year after my divorce, I was so sex affirmative and in love with life that it was the most natural thing in the world for me to say, "Of course! I'm going to create magnificent drawings of people celebrating sexual love." I began to transfer my experiences in bed onto paper. That decision turned out to be an important one. As a creative person, I'd consistently struggled against social restrictions and censorship. However, the worst repression was the kind of censorship I'd been taught to apply to myself: "What will

people think?" Once I put my sexual ideas down on paper, I was letting go of self-censorship, embracing a much larger concept of freedom to express myself.

I went public with my erotic art in 1968. It was my first one-woman exhibition and was held in a prestigious New York gallery. Naturally, the idea of displaying my interest in sex publicly generated an enormous amount of fear. I envisioned irate citizens throwing rocks through the gallery window or my getting busted for pornography. But I also knew that every new adventure in my life had always been preceded by fear. So instead of not wanting to be afraid, I put my arms around fear like I was hugging an old friend, and we went arm in arm to the opening. I needn't have worried. My large charcoal drawings of classical nudes making love behind sheets of brightly colored Plexiglas created a sensation. My heterosexual erotic art was quite acceptable. The exhibition was a beautiful and enormously successful event.

The gallery was on the block next to the Whitney Museum,

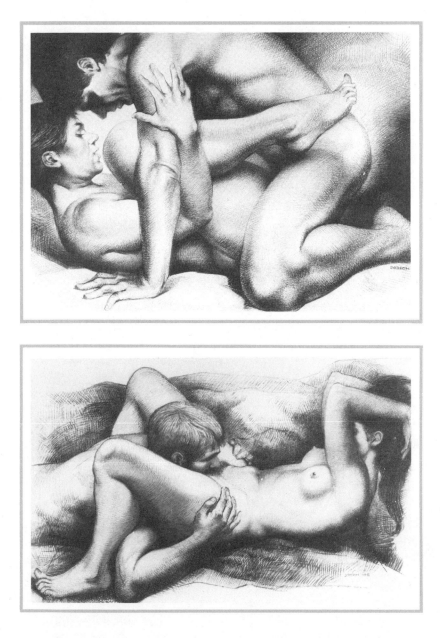

a perfect location. Even though advertising was largely word-of-mouth, over eight thousand people attended the exhibition in a two-week period—the largest number the gallery had ever recorded. There were many incidents that were funny, embarrassing, exciting, and also sad, but all of them were profoundly educational. One mother got halfway into the room with her ten-year-old daughter before she realized what the show was about. Obviously, she had missed the sign on the door. "Oh my," she gasped. "We don't want to look at these pictures!" "Why not, Mother? It's just a bunch of people wrestling," the child said, but she was whisked out of the gallery.

One fact was undeniable: people were interested in sex. The erotic art triggered many visitors into giving me mini sex histories. I was sharing a new kind of intimacy with complete strangers. It was a rich and rewarding experience that included many blessed moments of liberating truth.

One important insight I had was that women were more willing to exchange sex information than men. At the gallery women talked about their fears and hangups, and they asked lots of questions. Men were less open; they mostly made jokes and acted cool. Somehow men were supposed to have gained enough sexual expertise to teach women about sex. But having to project a masculine image at all times kept them from learning. If you already know all the answers, you can't ask questions. I concluded from the experience that women have to lead the way to sexual freedom and expression.

After hearing so many personal stories, I also discovered that nearly everyone was affected by socially imposed sex-negative attitudes. Many of these sex histories dealt with unnecessary pain and suffering, often from simple lack of information. I became more convinced than ever that masturbation was crucial to women's liberation. The bottom line of repression was our inability to touch our own bodies for sexual pleasure.

In a moment of divine madness, I decided to devote my second exhibition to selflove. I had visions of the redemption of masturbation in my fashionable Madison Avenue gallery. Everyone said I was nuts because the drawings would never sell. They were absolutely right! But it was an invaluable experience in raising my sexual consciousness.

Getting models to masturbate for me was a lot more difficult than getting couples to pose had been, which was an illuminating commentary in itself. Finally, with a little help from my friends, I got it down on paper. I completed four life-size classical nudes, two males and two females, all joyfully masturbating to orgasm. I thought they were beautiful. But when the drawings arrived at the gallery the day of the opening, all hell broke loose. The director refused to hang the four nudes as planned, so I threatened to pull the whole show. After an exhausting argument, two of the masturbation drawings were hung. It was clear that exhibiting drawings of people "jacking and jilling off" was going to cause problems. Why was selflove so terrifying?

That night, the main wall in the front room of this elegant establishment held the six-foot drawing of my girlfriend Nicole, legs apart, clitoris erect, approaching orgasm with her electric vibrator. Actually, she usually masturbated wearing her stereo earphones and enjoyed penetration using a peeled cucumber along with her vibrator, but for artistic purposes, I'd simplified her technique. And in the adjoining room, there was the second six-foot drawing of my boyfriend Adam, legs apart, penis erect, approaching orgasm by hand.

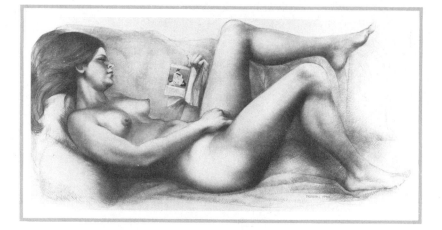

The response to this show was even more fascinating and informative than the response to the first one. A lot of women said they never masturbated. Men who admitted they masturbated made it clear they would rather "get laid." Some men didn't know women ever masturbated, while others were turned on by the idea of watching a woman "do herself." Men got into the drawing of the woman but quickly went past the one of the man, while women looked at both pictures. The vibrator made several men hostile and competitive. One virile stud said emphatically, "If that was my woman, she wouldn't have to use *that thing!*" In response, I encouraged cooperation instead of competition. It was like competing with the electric company, which seldom has power failures. Besides, an electric vibrator was available twenty-four hours a day.

Fielding hundreds of questions, I assured people that masturbation was healthy. "No, you don't get warts." "Yes, the woman with the vibrator in the picture has a boyfriend—he's standing right over there next to her." "No, despite what society tells us, intercourse isn't necessarily better, it's just different." "No, masturbation doesn't eliminate the desire for partnersex, it enhances it." "Yes, I do both and love it all."

Some of the stories I heard, in which people were severely

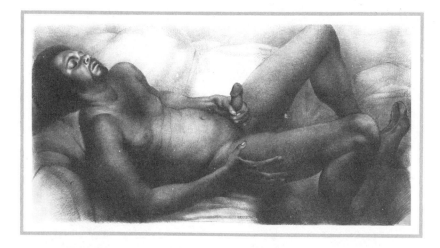

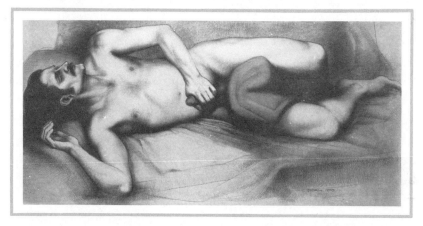

punished for childhood masturbation, brought tears to my eyes. A woman told me about an incident when she was seven years old. Her mother came in to kiss her goodnight, sniffed her daughter's fingers, and slapped her face, saying, "It smells like you've had your hand in a garbage pail!" The woman confessed that to this day, she was still unable to touch her genitals, and she was always uncomfortable when her husband touched them. She'd never experienced an orgasm during twenty years of marriage, though she loved her husband dearly.

The exhibition was held in 1970, and the vibrator revolution hadn't yet gotten under way, so many women I talked with had never heard of using an electric massage machine for sex. When I described it, every woman was convinced she'd be instantly addicted. I explained that although I loved my vibrator, I was still involved with "regular sex." My observation had been that women who liked vibrators also liked sex or were starting to enjoy sex for the first time.

If I had any doubts before, the two weeks I spent in the gallery made it clear that sexual repression related directly to the repression of masturbation. It followed then that masturbation could be important in reversing sexual repression.

Seeking sexual satisfaction is a basic desire, and masturbation is our first natural sexual activity. It's the way we discover our eroticism, the way we learn to respond sexually, the way we learn to love ourselves and to build self-esteem. Sexual skill and the ability to respond are not "natural" in our society. "Doing what comes naturally," is to be sexually inhibited. Sex, like any other skill, has to be learned and practiced. When a woman masturbates, she learns to like her own genitals, to enjoy her orgasms, and furthermore, to become proficient in sex. But some people are made very uncomfortable by the idea of a sexually proficient and independent woman.

In spite of a sexual revolution, the pill, and the women's movement, the sexual double standard is still alive and well. Men continue to have social approval to be sexually assertive, independent, and experienced, while women are expected to be sexually passive, dependent, and inexperienced. Fixed in nonsexuality and a supporting role, most women seek security rather than new experiences and sexual gratification.

The way women are made to conform to this double standard is through the deprivation of sexual self-knowledge. Deprived of their own bodies, they have no way of discovering or developing sexual responses. At an early age, women are prohibited from touching their genitals with the threat of supernatural or real punishment. Information about the clitoris and life-affirming orgasm is withheld, and women are instilled with the idea that female genitals are inferior; that a woman's main value lies in procreation and giving a man sexual pleasure. Without any sexual pleasure of her own, a woman may come to think of her genitals as being repulsive and a constant source of discomfort and shame. This kind of sexual repression is a vital aspect of keeping women in their "proper role."

The most insidious part of this system is that we women end up accepting the male definition of "normal" female sexuality. We are taught to maintain the two sexual views of women— Madonna or Whore—by socially ostracizing all nonconforming women. When we put down masturbation and overt displays of healthy female sexuality, we embellish our pedestals to become the next generation of the Keepers of Social Morality. The Matriarchy is the necessary support system and moral police force for the Patriarchy.

I was overwhelmed with the full realization of how effectively women had been turned into sexless mothers and docile house slaves. Feeling the enormity of the sexual damage done to women, I started calling every woman I knew and loved, asking each one if she was joyfully masturbating. If she was, I gave her encouragement to continue, and if she wasn't, I suggested she start immediately! It was my first telephone campaign to get women's sexual liberation underway.

One of those calls was long distance to Kansas—to my mother. At that time, she was sixty-nine and living alone, a widow of several years. I started right off with "Mother, are you masturbating to orgasm?" There was a sputtering pause, and then she answered, "Why, Betty Ann, of course not! I'm too old for that sort of thing." I immediately launched into my whole rap about the connection between good health and orgasm. If nothing else, she could do it as a physical exercise to keep the lining of the vaginal wall lubricating, the hormones secreting, and the uterus contracting. Besides, it was a great way to relax and unwind. It might possibly reduce her lower back pains. She could also do it just for fun!

This time there was a long, thoughtful pause.

"Well, honey, I don't know. What you say does make sense. You always have such different ideas from most people, but I think you're probably right."

Our next conversation two weeks later was wonderful! Yes, she'd successfully and easily masturbated to orgasm. Mother said it had been pleasant, and she felt that afterward she'd slept more soundly. Then she chuckled and said it could never compare with the "real thing."

That phone call opened up our sexual dialogue, which had been silent for nearly twenty years. We gradually began to include sex talk in our conversations, exchanging information about masturbation and even sharing our masturbation histories. She had masturbated regularly as a child. While she was going with my father, she often masturbated after a date because she was so turned on. This way she maintained her virginity until her wedding night. After marriage, she never masturbated again. One surprise for me: she remembered my masturbating in the backseat of the car when I was five years old and we were on our way to California. At the time I didn't think about the rearview mirror and had no idea she knew. Why hadn't she stopped me? "That was such a long trip," she explained. "You were having fun, and I didn't want to bother you." She associated masturbation with harmless pleasure from her own childhood experiences. My love and gratitude for her were very real. I'd been raised by an orgasmic mother.

One time I asked Mother if she ever talked about masturbation with any of her friends. She said yes, a friend of hers was complaining about a terrible vaginal itch that the doctor had been unable to cure. Mother suggested that masturbation might help. Her friend stopped calling after that conversation. Mother decided never to bring up the subject again; people were just too ignorant. I totally supported her. Enjoying her own orgasms was her personal sexual revolution, and it was quite enough. Not only did society try to pretend that women had modest sex drives, it also made sex for older people seem obscene or abnormal. I gave Mother a lot of credit for repudiating the myth, and I openly acknowledged her as a radical feminist, which she loved.

Raising
Sexual
Consciousness

By making no secret of my sexlife and laughing away myths about masturbation, I began to feel more self-confident. Sexual honesty was very healing, and I was committed to telling my women friends what I'd been learning through my own efforts to change. Going public about sex brought letters, phone calls, and questions from women of varied backgrounds, all wanting to know more about selflove and orgasm. Sharing sex information was another step in raising my sexual consciousness. Women communicating with women about sex was reversing the repression conditioned so deeply into the female psyche. Finally I understood perfectly that *the personal was political.* If women could learn to share information about their sexlives, feminism would be a major event in sexual history.

A classic case of repressed female masturbation was that of my friend Nancy. At the age of twenty-five, after six years of sexual intercourse, she wasn't sure if she'd ever experienced an orgasm. (It's hard to imagine a young man with a similar problem!) I felt the only way she'd know for sure was to learn how to bring herself to orgasm. Nancy had never consciously masturbated. I described some of the sensations I'd experienced and drew a picture of the female genitals, explaining the importance of the clitoris.

After a week, Nancy admitted that she felt silly and self-conscious trying to masturbate. Furthermore, nothing had happened. When I discovered she'd only spent ten minutes on her selfloving, I gently pointed out that she devoted hours to her face and hair. It might be worth it to spend at least an hour on her body.

Then I went into more detail describing several different hand techniques, emphasizing how sensuous everything would feel with massage oil. She could use one or more fingers or the flat of her hand, moving in circles, up and down, or from side to side. She could try rubbing her pubic mound or pressing her outer lips together. She could touch her clitoris directly or on either side, varying the rhythm and the amount of pressure. I also suggested that she read a sexy book or try to have a sexual fantasy.

"Still nothing," Nancy reported several weeks later. She complained that her hand had gotten tired, and she was bored with the whole exercise. I recommended a vibrator, but she rejected the idea as "too mechanical." Then I remembered another friend who'd experienced her first orgasm in the bathtub by letting the water run on her genitals. She'd been too inhibited to touch herself "there," and she said the water was like a spiritual lover caressing her. I passed this information along to Nancy, and it worked. Orgasm at last! This time there was no doubt in her mind. She was thrilled that it had finally happened and also furious that it had taken her so long. I reminded her of several women we knew who didn't have orgasms until they were in their forties.

For the next six months, Nancy was "going steady" with her bathtub until she got over her mechanical reservations and purchased an electric vibrator. Now she could have orgasms in her bedroom. She'd also just started a new love affair and was confused about whether to tell her boyfriend that she'd never climaxed from intercourse. I urged her to get him involved in her sexual unfolding immediately, stressing the importance of not faking orgasm. "Once we fake it, we're trapped in the biggest sexual lie of all," I said. To Nancy's delight, her boyfriend was more than happy to be included. The night she got up enough courage to bring out her vibrator, they had a marvelous "threesome." Within a short time, Nancy could have orgasms during intercourse using her vibrator or when her lover did oralsex. She was in heaven!

Seeing what communication between women could mean, I was ready to become a card-carrying feminist. I joined NOW, but at the time it seemed too conservative. Next I went to a women's center started by younger, more radical women. A woman at the desk said the center had no CR (consciousness-raising) groups available and suggested I start one of my own. My immediate response was, "But I have no experience." According to her, my experience of being a woman more than qualified me. I wanted some kind of guidelines, a manual, anything, but all I got was a smile and confident advice: "Just get the women together, and let it happen."

Still hung up about who was going to lead the group, I asked two friends to help me. We set up a night and called women we thought would be interested. Between nine and fifteen of us met once a week for over a year. Experimenting with different formats and topics, we shared our information, strength, and hope with one another. It created a powerful new learning environment. Being in an all-woman group on a regular basis connected me to lost childhood memories. In my youth, I always had close girlfriends whom I loved. But I'd been systematically diverted from loving girls as I grew older and socially rewarded when I loved boys. As a grown woman, I knew there was always a potential sexual implication when women were together on a regular basis, and the word *lesbian* terrified me. I had enough problems without being a sexual deviant. Looking back, I could see how sexually timid I'd been. But thanks to my erotic evolution, I became bolder and more experimental.

In the late sixties, when sexparties were flourishing, I'd discovered the joys of having playful sex with women. This new erotic dimension felt natural to me, and I started calling myself "bisexual." I loved the freedom of allowing myself to feel attracted to both sexes.

Then along came the in-fighting between the heterosexual and lesbian feminists in the early seventies. Identifying myself as a bisexual feminist meant I couldn't make up my mind. But I didn't want to be a pure lesbian and repress my erotic feelings toward men any more than I wanted to be a pure heterosexual and repress my erotic feelings toward women. I felt like a little androgynous elf scampering between the two opposing camps, extolling the pleasures of selflove and masturbation.

When I started having my first ongoing sexual relationship with a woman, I was again confronted with an either/or situation. According to society, women could either be romantic lesbian lovers or Platonic heterosexual friends. By combining the best of both possibilities, Laura and I became *sexual friends*. It was a new erotic category for bisexual women.

Laura was one of the bravest young women I'd ever met. A corporate banker by day and a radical feminist by night, she was a skilled martial artist who walked the streets without fear. She was also a classic beauty with piercing hazel eyes. She had just turned thirty, and I was forty-two, so I often felt like a big sister who was more experienced, especially in sexual matters.

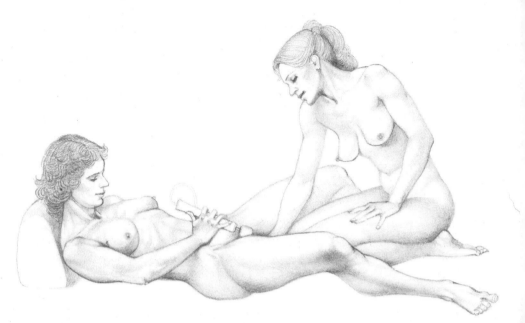

During our many discussions about feminism, I explained my sexual politics to Laura. I thought compulsive monogamy, idealized romantic love, and dependent sex were the combined curse of womankind. To avoid these things, I felt it was important for both of us to spend time apart. She agreed, and all the time we were together, we continued to have other sexual and Platonic friends.

Gradually we evolved a sexual sharing that pleased both of us. Laura's Catholic upbringing had made sex a misery. Only recently had she learned how to have an orgasm with masturbation. At first when we tried oralsex, it made us both feel anxious. Laura felt pressured to perform when I did her, and I worried about taking too long when she did me. We let go of trying to give each other an orgasm and shared masturbation instead.

Massage and masturbation gave us a surprising amount of sexual variety. Some nights we did massage only and experienced the joy of no sex. Other times we took turns heightening each other's orgasms by combining massage with masturbation. One

47

of us would use a vibrator while the other one would do sensuous touching and vaginal or anal penetration. There were other
times when we would use the same vibrator simultaneously. The
one on the bottom held the vibrator in the position that was
good for her while the one on top had to move around to get
what she wanted. We always took turns leading or following.

Sharing masturbation was very healing, and we ended up
exchanging hundreds of hours of massage. Instead of being stuck
with a romantic image of sex, Laura and I were sharing an erotic
image of love. When we finally parted, our love didn't turn into
hate, and our meaningful friendship goes on to this day.

During the time Laura and I were evolving our sexual friendship, I joined a new CR group comprised of professional women
who wanted to set up a strong support system, an "old-girls"
network for women interested in money and power. I, of course,

advocated power that was based on pleasure. Economic power wasn't enough. Without sexual liberation, which freed the human spirit, we would misuse power in the same way as men had. A ruling matriarchy was no different from a patriarchy—they were two sides of the same coin that represented the family. Both Mother and Father were dictators, benevolent or cruel. In my family, Daddy was a pushover, but Mother was a force to be reckoned with.

One night during a meeting in my new CR group, I talked at length about my sexlife, hoping to start a sexual dialogue. I shared what I'd observed during the time I'd gone to sexparties. Many women were faking orgasms. The men were coming, and the women were pleasing their partners. I felt that a woman couldn't really love herself if her sexlife was based on pretending. I went on to say that I also enjoyed having sex with both men and women. Although I considered myself to be a bisexual feminist, I thought it was important to embrace all the labels to diffuse their impact. People were socially tortured by having to choose between being straight or gay. Until sex labels became obsolete, I was going to call myself a heterosexual bisexual lesbian. When I finished my rap, the room was silent.

I was shocked to discover that the personal wasn't political, not when it came to sex. Everyone felt that sex was a private matter, while I thought it was a top-priority feminist issue. Among the women in the group there were several writers and editors, a photographer, a television producer, a film writer, a theater director, an actress, and two corporate vice presidents. Only two were married—the rest of us were divorced or single. Automatically, I'd assumed career women would be more open-minded sexually, more independent. It wasn't true. Job insecurities and financial problems still made finding the right man the emotional bedrock of security. There was nothing wrong with wanting to share love, sex, and money with a partner. But I felt selflove had to come first.

Patience was my middle name as I sat and listened to painful, repetitive stories of love addiction. Being properly brought up and well-educated, these beautiful women were trapped in false modesty and very uptight about their bodies. They all had drippy romantic attitudes about sex, and it was causing them a lot of unhappiness and conflict. I suspected that most of them were hooked on trying to get all their orgasms from intercourse. Everyone in the group was exclusively heterosexual. Whenever I talked about my bisexuality, which I called "the natural condition," they all tensed up with their own fears of lesbianism. But I continued to discuss my sexlife while they laughed nervously and humored me. They all agreed that I was from another planet while I kept assuring them I was from Kansas.

Nonetheless, I loved these intelligent women. After all, they were "normal," according to society. I was the one who was on the fringe of sexual behavior. Once a week I couldn't wait to get to my CR group to be a sexual clown, a mime, and a sister-teacher. I did sexual assertiveness training with them on how to ask a man out on a date and how to get what they wanted sexually. I also demonstrated how to reach down and stimulate a clitoris during intercourse, and of course I raved about guilt-free masturbation and showed them different pelvic movements and positions I used with my vibrator. They all gasped that night I took off my shirt and flexed my little biceps while I talked about the importance of developing our bodies in order to be better in bed.

Most important, I made them laugh! We laughed together for hours, week after week, month after month. They were horrified, amused, embarrassed, tickled, and finally grateful. Eventually I discovered that most of them were having secret orgasms with masturbation when they were alone and faking orgasms when they were with their lovers. Before I left the group, I bought a case of high-powered electric vibrators and passed them out, assuring them that a sexually turned-on woman was a joy to a man, not a threat. Some of the vibrators got hidden in the back of closets, but the courageous women made the vibrator and masturbation an integral part of their sexlives.

Female sexual repression wasn't going to disappear overnight just because that's what I wanted to happen. I'd signed up for the longest revolution—women's liberation. In 1920 we'd gotten the vote, and now we were working on the Equal Rights Amendment. If everything moved that slowly, I felt that 1973 wasn't a moment too soon to kick off the Equal Orgasms Amendment. The idea of giving up my career as an artist to become a sex teacher was both exciting and terrifying. But I had no degrees. How could I teach? Then I remembered that my experience of being a woman more than qualified me. I just had to get the women together and let it happen.

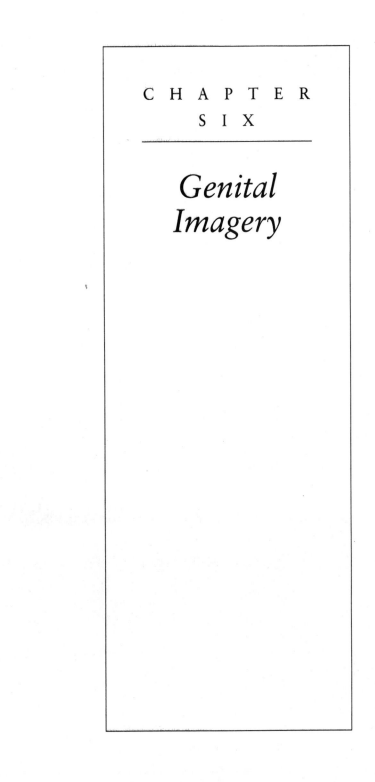

CHAPTER SIX

Genital Imagery

*A*round the age of ten, I wanted to see what I looked like "down there." One afternoon when the house was empty, I got Mother's hand mirror and went into my bedroom. Sitting by the window with sunlight pouring in, I looked at my sweet little child's genitals and was instantly horrified. There hanging down were the same funny-looking things that dangled from a chicken's neck. Right on the spot, I swore off masturbation and made a deal with God. If He got rid of those things that hung down, I promised to stop playing with myself, keep my room clean, and love my little brothers.

After a couple of weeks of abstinence, which wasn't easy, I examined my genital deformity again. Upon more careful observation, I saw that my left inner lip was shorter than the right one. I cleverly decided to switch sides and continue playing with myself until they evened up, and *then* stop forever. Throughout the rest of my childhood, into adulthood, I masturbated with my finger on the left side of my genitals. My inner lips never evened up or dropped off. I simply kept the knowledge of my genital deformity to myself. It was just another one of the many things wrong with me, and I quietly settled into confirmed body loathing.

At the age of thirty-five, I still had an ugly mental image of my genitals. In the past, men had "gone down" on me, but I was always much too uncomfortable to reach an orgasm. The thought of someone tasting my genitals struck me as being unsanitary. Worse yet, he might see everything. I could only allow oralsex to continue for a few moments before I pulled my lover back up on top of me for "normal sex."

After I got divorced, I was determined to try everything. Blake introduced me to oralsex as a main event, not just foreplay. I quickly discovered that my orgasms for oral lovemaking were very intense. Once, after a profound climax, he said, "You have a beautiful cunt. Let me look at you under the light." He reached for his glasses, and I almost died. I quickly said, "I'd appreciate it if you didn't." Then I thought to myself, What kind of a sick, perverted nut wants to look anyway? Evidently I'd turned a bit green, because he wanted to know what was the matter. I confessed to having stretched my inner lips. He looked at me in disbelief. Then he put his arms around me and said, "Honey, you're perfectly normal. A lot of women are made like that. Actually, it's one of my favorite styles."

Lucky for me he was a devoted appreciator of the female genitals, a connoisseur of cunts. Off he went to a closet, coming back with a stack of magazines. They were soft-core porn that featured "split beaver." "Beaver" was a slang expression for female genitals, and "split beaver" was the term used when a woman held her genitals open. I was shocked but interested. How degrading for those poor women to pose in garter belts and black net stockings, exposing themselves like this, I thought. Nonetheless, I began looking at the photographs, and sure enough, there was a vulva just like mine, and another, and another. By the time we'd gone through several magazines together, I knew what women's genitals looked like. What a relief! In that one session, I discovered that I wasn't deformed or ugly. I couldn't get over it! All those years of therapy hadn't made a dent in my body loathing. No wonder I'd never liked oralsex and always wanted to make love in the dark. Just thirty minutes of viewing pornography had started my process of becoming "cunt positive," which changed my life.

Not long after that, I painted my first genital self-portrait. While posing for myself in front of my makeup mirror, I was flabbergasted to realize that all those years I had drawn the nude, women's genitals were never more than a triangle of hair. It was just another example of the degree of my own sexual ignorance and lack of self-knowledge. What a difference it would have made in my self-image and sexual development if I could have seen pretty pictures of adult genitals in a sex book.

At first, I disliked the word *cunt*. It was only used as a derogatory term. When men said it in anger, I heard it with fear and disgust. But when a lover said it with passion, it sounded sexy. Most women said *vagina,* but technically that was the passageway leading from the external genitalia to the uterus. *Vulva* was more accurate; it referred to the outer and inner lips and the cleft between. But that sounded like a car: "I get great mileage with my Vulva." *Pudenda* also meant the external genitalia, but it was rather heavy—"My Pedantic Pudenda." Though I was a cat lover, *pussy* was too euphemistic and reduced me to the status of household pet. I would have to use *female genitals* exclusively, unless I got up enough nerve to use the gutsy old Anglo-Saxon noun *cunt*. One inspired day, I looked into the mirror and repeated out loud, "Cunt, cunt, cunt . . . ," about a hundred times until I started laughing. The word no longer held a negative power over me. In continuing the process of becoming positive about my genitals I started using the word *cunt* in my writing and speech.

In 1973, I joined with other feminists to plan the first NOW Conference on Women's Sexuality. During one of our early meetings, a friend asked, "What would you like to do for the plenary session?" Quite spontaneously I answered, "I want to do a slide show of split beaver for feminists." Almost everyone broke up laughing. For the benefit of two women, I had to explain "split beaver" was porno slang. One woman thought it was a very derogatory male term. I assured her that I would come up with a suitable name and produce the slides. In the conference flyer, it was called "Creating an Aesthetic for the Female Genitals," which was the academic way of saying "Becoming Cunt Positive." I didn't care what we called it as long as I got to do it.

I started calling friends, asking if they would like to pose for the first feminist pornography. The response was positive and about twenty women plus two women photographers met at my apartment. It was a fantastic gathering. The lights and camera were set up in the bedroom, and in the living room, the women chatted while they trimmed and shaped their pubic hair in prepa-ration for their cunt portraits. We took turns posing with our genitals in a natural position, the outer lips held open, and one exposing the clitoris. Then each of us was given a mirror and asked to arrange our genitals in the way we thought they looked most appealing.

There were "oohs" and "ahhs" and other comments such as, "How beautiful," "Look at the pretty mother-of-pearl texture," and "What exquisite coloring." Occasionally there would be a spontaneous round of applause when a woman displayed herself artfully. We began to see designs, shapes, patterns, and made associations with nature: a shell, a flower, a fig, an orchid, and yes, even those dangling wattles (I now think chickens are sexy). I saw styles emerging: there was a Classical Cunt with symmetry, a Baroque style with complex folds and drapery, a Gothic Cunt with archways, and a Danish Modern with clean lines. There were many Valentine Cunts. When we realized the heart design was the shape of a woman's genitals when she held her outer vaginal lips open, St. Valentine's Day suddenly had a new meaning.

We discovered that when the hood was pulled back and each clitoris appeared, the variations were astounding—ranging from tiny little seed pearls to rather large protruding jewels. In the dictionary *phallus* refers to both the penile glans and the clitoral glans. We were changing our image from the Female Eunuch to the Phallic Woman. The distance of the clitoris from the vaginal opening also varied greatly. One woman with a clit close to her vagina said she could have orgasms with intercourse alone. I thought I'd discovered a new theory until a woman with the same configuration posed, and she said she always needed direct clitoral stimulation to have an orgasm. Another woman couldn't get her clitoris to pop out. She was convinced she didn't have one until she pressed a finger on either side of the clitoral shaft. We could just see the tip of her shy clit. Technically called an "embedded clitoris," it was difficult to see, but it was easy to feel and worked just fine.

The vaginal opening wasn't a hole at all, but rather soft little pink folds that created different patterns in each woman. We became aware of the differences in pubic hair and genital coloring. Some women had dark, thick bushes and others fine, wispy hair. One woman shaved off her pubic hair, and she was our Futuristic Cunt. The form of her genitals were stark and beautiful. Our colors ranged from pale pink to dark brown, and one woman had a two-tone cunt. Her inner lips were dark brown surrounded by a delicate peach. Another woman who had very dark brown genitals and black pubic hair said her lover called her "The Black Orchid."

Throughout the evening there was animated conversation. There were also moments of silence as each of us became lost in our own thoughts. Toward the end, I closed my eyes and saw one exquisite cunt after another pass before my mind's eye. We were creating our own genital imagery—not the male version of "pussies" and "beavers," but the women's version of the lotus flower unfolding for the new Aquarian Age.

I showed the slides to over a thousand women at the NOW conference. When the lights went back on, there was a long standing ovation. Goose bumps covered my body as I had an emotional orgasm with my multitude of lovers. Afterward many

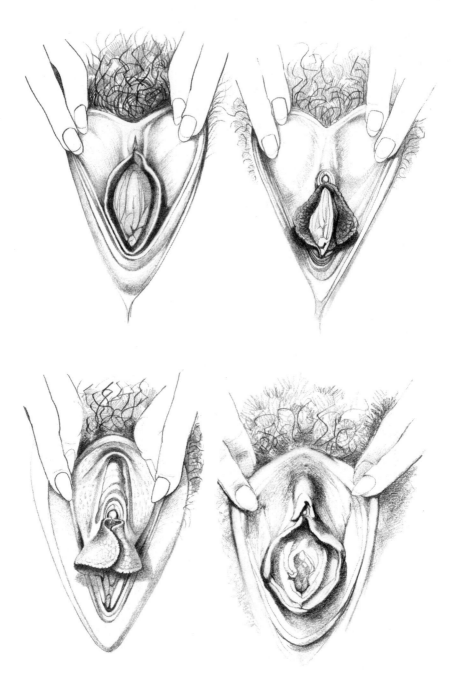

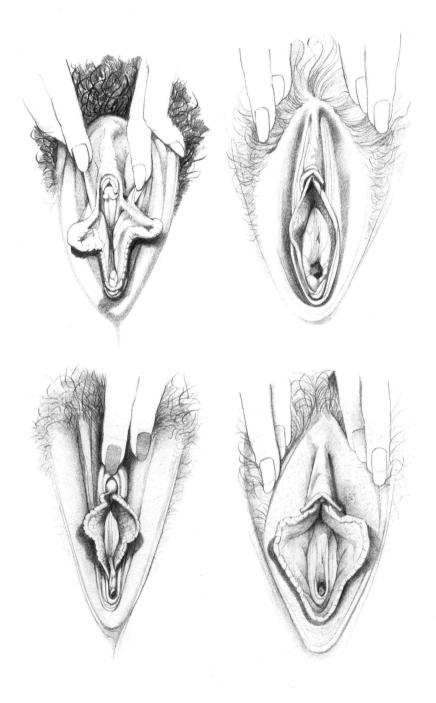

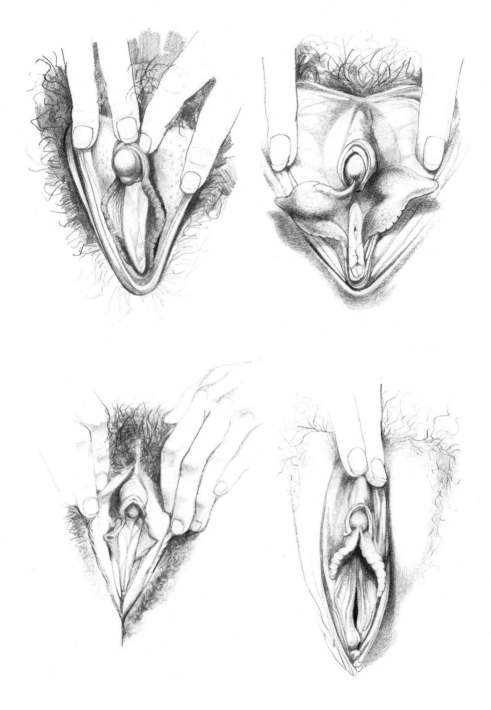

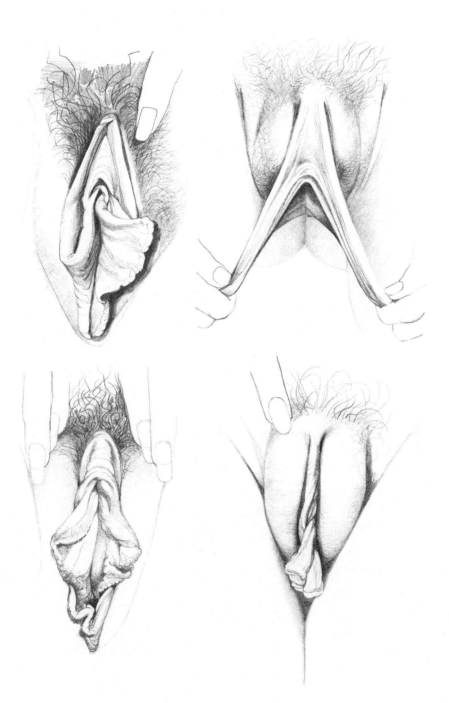

women gave me enthusiastic feedback. Several told me they felt dramatically changed by looking at the slides. Others said they, too, had thought they were deformed. One woman asked her boss for a raise the next day—and got it! Becoming cunt positive had enhanced her self-worth and she felt she deserved more money.

A year later, I did a series of pen-and-ink drawings from the slides for *Liberating Masturbation* and included them in the slide show, along with a picture of a shell, an orchid, and a jade cunt necklace. I felt it was such important visual information for women that I made myself say yes to every lecture request. Traveling around the country, I carried a slide carousel filled with images of the Temple Priestesses Sacred Clits or pornographic split beaver, depending on a person's point of view. The difference between porn and erotica was definitely in the eyes of the beholder. I showed my female genital slide show in New York, New Jersey, Connecticut, Florida, Kansas, Colorado, and California. University students, women's groups, and many sex educators all had the opportunity to become cunt positive. After saying the word thousands of times with love from all the different podiums, I felt I had reclaimed the word *cunt*. Germaine Greer said it first in an article I'd read in 1969 titled, "Lady, Love Your Cunt."

By the late seventies, female genital imagery was emerging in women's art. Until then, Georgia O'Keeffe's flowers were just flowers. She herself denied her floral paintings represented vulvas. Then Judy Chicago and company blew the art world's mind with *The Dinner Party*. Many of her thirty-nine ceramic plates were designs of gorgeous cunts. A number of unknown women artists sent me slides of their paintings of cunts, including genital self-portraits that were inspired by my pen-and-ink drawings. I also received a lovely stained-glass piece that was fashioned after the decorative cunt drawing on the cover of my book *Liberating Masturbation*. At one point, I halfway expected to see cunt designs on sheets and towels. A friend who was a textile designer made an interesting repeat of decorative vaginas for wallpaper, but it never sold. What did become popular was genital jewelry. Pretty little cunts and cocks made out of silver, gold, glass, and ceramic graced many ears, fingers and necks. I even bought an erotic potholder made by a craftswoman who had stitched an adorable cunt in the middle.

A few new college textbooks on sex have included genital imagery, discussing the differences in both male and female genital forms. But very little has been done on the high-school level, where it's most needed, with young kids developing sexually so early. We will be more civilized and humane when beautiful genital imagery along with a positive attitude about masturbation is part of the sex education of every American boy and girl. Now and then there are signs of progress though. Just the other day I saw a friend's teenage daughter wearing a shocking-pink button that said, VIVA LA VULVA.

When everyone grows up with positive images of cunts and cocks, no one will secretly think herself or himself as genitally deformed. It's especially important for women to see genital imagery that includes the clitoris. Once a woman understands the role her clitoris plays in her sexual pleasure, she can always show her lover how to stimulate her to orgasm.

I once read a letter in one of the popular sex magazines addressed to the doctor's column that sent me into a rage. Under the heading "Large Vaginal Lips," a twenty-year-old woman said she recently noticed that her inner lips seemed to have gotten very large. She wanted to know if masturbating could have caused it and what should she do? The doctor answered that large inner lips are in part hereditary, and ". . . if, as a part of your masturbating, you pull on the labia minora, you could of course stretch and lengthen them. If the labia are so enlarged as to trouble you or make you feel too embarrassed to attempt intercourse, it's a relatively simple procedure to reduce the size." He went on to recommend a trip to the doctor's office, a little Novocaine, and snip, snip—off come the offenders. I shall refrain from calling this doctor a dirty name and simply point out that he was not cunt positive.

Another offensive medical recommendation is the clitorotomy, or female circumcision. A friend of mine, who was orgasmic with a vibrator only, longed to have orgasms from her lover's penis. She consulted her doctor, who told her that if some of the hood was removed from her clitoris, it might be more sensitive, allowing her to climax with intercourse. He only suggested the surgery "might help." It was a simple office procedure—a little Novocaine, and snip, snip. She had her circumcision and got an infection, which added two more weeks to the ordeal. When she recovered, she still couldn't reach orgasm from penetration alone. In my opinion, male or female circumcision is an unnecessary surgical procedure.

It's time to stop insisting on the Romantic Ideal of having all of our orgasms from Romeo's cock inside Juliet's cunt! If a woman can stimulate herself to orgasm, she's orgasmic. "Frigid" is a man's word for a woman who can't have an orgasm in the missionary position in a few minutes with only the kind of stimulation that's good for him. The truth is, very few women consistently reach orgasm in intercourse without additional stimulation. (Imagine a man trying to have an orgasm without touching the head of his cock!) We don't always have to come to enjoy sex, but a woman who's not achieving orgasm most of the time cannot possibly maintain a joyful attitude toward sex over an extended period of time.

The crucial role of the clitoris has been established. Nowadays, well-recognized sex clinics and sex therapists use masturbation therapy to help women and men to develop long-suppressed sexual response patterns. In spite of the recent "G-Spot" theory that got women searching for a magic place inside the vagina to trigger orgasm, the clitoris remains our principal sex organ. So far, I haven't been able to find my "G-Spot." Looking for it reminded me of the role Linda Lovelace played in the porno movie *Deep Throat*: she thought her clitoris was that little thing that hung down from the roof of her mouth, definitely a male fantasy of female sexual response. But then I have a couple of friends who love their "G-Spots" and that's great.

Vaginal penetration is very erotic, especially when it's done with design and sensitivity. Both the exterior and interior parts of our genitalia produce lovely sensations. Some women prefer orgasms from penetration only; others want direct clitoral stimulation during intercourse; and some women prefer oralsex. Then there are those women, like myself, who want it all, including masturbation.

My obsession with women's liberation was so all consuming that for a decade I didn't think about the importance of men becoming cock positive. I just assumed most men liked their penises, especially with all the privileges that went with owning one. But I was wrong. Feeling bad about one's body and genitals isn't restricted to women. Sexual repression affects both sexes.

When a man enjoys masturbation and feels good about his sexlife, he will like his penis. But for a man suffering from impotence, his penis is a source of great disappointment. Or a penis can be a constant cause of terrible temptation for a religious celibate or a monogamous husband. Castration images and fantasies are the result of extreme penis hatred. Castration fears probably stem from the repression of male masturbation. The little boy happily playing with his pecky gets traumatized when his mother threatens to cut it off if he doesn't stop.

When Blake was married and taking pills to fight off depression, he said his cock was a constant reminder of his sexual frustration. Though he loved his wife, his heart ached for sexual adventures. He couldn't even enjoy masturbation for fear of getting caught. At one point he got so angered that he actually imagined putting his penis on the window ledge and slamming the window shut. That castration fantasy occurred to him more than once.

After Blake got divorced and had a few flings, there was a dramatic change in the relationship he had with his cock. He went for days, it seemed, holding on to it, free at last to masturbate any time he felt like it. Recently, at the age of sixty-three, he photographed his penis in a state of full erection and airmailed his cock portrait to one of his girlfriends in Michigan. The caption read "thinking of you."

I think a lot of heterosexual men take their cocks for granted, unless they're built very small or very large. The man with a little cock most likely wants a bigger one unless he's learned how to be a great lover, in which case size is unimportant. The man with a giant cock impresses other men but the large size of his organ can frighten off many women.

With the exception of a few men and women who have a thing about big dorks, most of us are satisfied and fulfilled with a medium-size penis. I don't know if there's scientific data about what size range constitutes the norm, but my guess is between five and seven inches erect, measured from the top. That doesn't mean that a man with four inches or nine inches can't be cock positive. It's not the size of the fish, it's the motion of the ocean.

Some cocks naturally curve upward and others can curve to the right or left. I've even seen a cock that curved downward. But none of these different directions interferes with good sex.

The thickness and length of the shaft varies in men as much as the clitoral shaft varies in women. It can be short or long, thick or thin. The shape, size, and color of the head on a cock also varies as much as clitorises do. The top of a penis can be pointed, flared around the edge, or shaped like a flattened knob.

The same as with cunts, there are Classical Cocks with symmetry, Baroque Cocks with complex folds and veins, and Danish Modern Cocks with clean lines. They come in an assortment of colors; beige, peach, brown, chocolate, lavender, and pink.

It's only one woman's dream, but I believe that when all men can really worship their phalluses, guns and MX missiles will become obsolete. Imagine a cunt- and cock-positive government running this great nation of ours.

CHAPTER
SEVEN

*The Bodysex
Groups*

After three years of consciousness-raising groups, I was burned out on cataloguing female suffering and social injustices. I was also tired of my romantic image of the "fine artist" isolated in her ivory-tower studio. Instead of struggling to solve aesthetic problems that I'd created, I wanted to help solve some social problems that already existed. Sex was a key feminist issue, it could either enslave or liberate us. My artist's spirit longed to replace feminist rhetoric with my feminist erotic images. I decided to set up physical and sexual consciousness-raising groups so women could creatively explore pleasure together.

I needed a special space for my new erotic project. In a moment of either madness or divine inspiration, I got rid of all the expensive furniture collected during my marriage. In one magnificent gesture, I let go of my cherished symbols of respectability and ended up with a big empty room. Friends looked on in amazement, and ~o did I. Out went Louis the Sixteenth and in came Betty the First, as I transformed my traditional living room into a Temple of Pleasure. I bought plush wall-to-wall carpeting and installed mirrors. On the walls, my erotic art went up, and over the fireplace I hung nude photos of me in yoga postures. With pillows placed around the room, the effect was one of elegance and spacious simplicity. I was in business.

In January of 1973, I started calling all the women I knew to recruit participants in the first Bodysex Workshops. I felt we could cover enough ground meeting one evening a week for four weeks. As I explained to each woman we were going to be in the nude, I could tell it was a threatening idea. But I only wanted to play with courageous women. My basic plan was to take a holistic view of our bodies and pleasure. We would do body movements including yoga and kung fu exercises, discuss food and health, perform genital examinations, share our masturbation histories, and describe our orgasms (or lack of orgasms). I was going to teach masturbation by demonstration and share my experience.

Realizing I would need help, I asked my friend Laura to assist me with the groups. She was delighted and gave an enthusiastic yes. For four years, Laura and I ran the workshops together. During the first year we had two separate groups a week. After each session, Laura and I would go over everything that happened in detail. Getting feedback from her was the support I needed.

Each workshop had its own group personality. Some were sexually reserved and verbal while others were sweet and sensuous. There was also the occasional group that was bawdy and outrageous. All of them were fun because Laura and I were such clowns.

The pleasure rituals came into being as the members of each group expressed their desires. There were suburban wives and mothers along with professional women who were married, divorced, or single. In age, we spanned the twenties through the fifties, with an occasional grandmother in her sixties. Most of the women were heterosexual, but in many of the groups there were also bisexuals and lesbians. I always made it clear that I supported all sexstyles. Focusing on selfsexuality and selflove took the emphasis off sexual labels. We were simply sexual women.

Since most women have no visual images of sex, I knew one demonstration would be worth a thousand words. At first I taught masturbation by doing pantomime, acting out what a buildup of sexual tension looked like, showing them how a body moved first with a mild orgasm and then an intense orgasm. That was always followed by a funny take-off on a porno star faking a hysterical thrashing orgasm. The homework every week was to practice masturbation. There were different kinds of vibrators available for the women who were interested in taking one home. It was such a cute assignment it made everyone laugh.

One night after I did the masturbation demonstration, a rather timid woman said she'd like to see a *real climax* some day. Spontaneously, Laura and I plugged in our vibrators and masturbated all the way to orgasm. When we finished, the group broke into cheers and applause. Our performance anxieties became a thing of the past after getting rave reviews from a few more groups. Talking about sex was very limiting. I knew we were doing first-rate teaching when live masturbation became a regular feature of the Bodysex Groups. The women were getting a visual image of sex with two different styles of orgasms. Laura's masturbation pattern was to have several smaller comes during the time it took me to have one bigger orgasm.

It was very reassuring for women to see Laura and me having authentic orgasms. Some women were not sure if they had ever had an orgasm because they didn't know what to look for. Watching us showed them the moves, the breathing, and they could see the energy. Several women who said they weren't orgasmic were mistaken. It turned out they were having little orgasms. After they saw us coming, they realized their idea of orgasm was very exaggerated. They expected a climax to be like a grand mal seizure.

When Laura and I demonstrated the different positions for sex, we had a running dialogue that poked fun at the sexroles. We would argue about who was going to play the part of the man and the woman. Then we would criticize each other's portrayal. Our male was clumsy and too aggressive while our female was prissy and too passive. The women loved our silliness. We demonstrated the right-angle position with the woman lying on her back and the man on his side. We also did the "missionary," "woman superior," "spoons," and "doggie" styles. In each position we emphasized clitoral stimulation by hand or vibrator while we simulated intercourse. Our erotic finale was showing how two women could use the same vibrator and dance their way to orgasm.

Much to my amazement, I quickly became a good facilitator and administrator. Within a year, I was doing groups on the West Coast and was being invited by feminists to run workshops in other parts of the country. My motto soon became, "Have vibrator, will travel." Although the temptation was great, and offers of financial backing were many, I resisted developing the Bodysex Groups into a big commercial operation. My gut feeling defied intellectual explanations. I just *knew* the groups had to remain an intimate experience *for me,* or they would lose their healing power.

I never advertised the groups, but word of mouth traveled fast. Women heard glowing reports from their friends and signed up. Some women admitted to waiting months, even years before they got up enough nerve to register. I didn't run the groups on a consistent basis, and I told myself that each year was the last. Thinking about doing more groups was always overwhelming. Feeling responsible for each woman's well-being was exhausting. However, the actual experience was so exhilarating that sooner or later I would get over my resistance and set up another round.

After five years the format finally evolved to two-day weekend groups with a maximum of fifteen women that I conducted alone. No one was ever pressured to do anything she didn't feel like doing. The first principle of pleasure was freedom of personal choice.

At the opening session, I would answer the door nude and greet each woman. They would undress immediately, which eliminated any extra time to worry about nudity. The thought was far more unnerving than the actual experience. Within the first hour, any embarrassment disappeared as everyone realized how natural it was to be in our bodies together. By the second session, the women couldn't wait to get their clothes off.

The circle, an ancient form for group communication, allowed us to sit in an equal position in full view of everyone. After lighting a candle in the center, I usually shared a current fantasy. For example, we were gathered to plan a takeover of Washington to eroticize the nation, or we were vibrator priestesses practicing for our performance at Carnegie Hall. Sitting in a cross-legged pose, we straightened our spines, leveled our chins, expanded rib cages, and instantly, we were magnificent! Before talking, we did a round or two of cleansing breathing to let go of any remaining tension.

Talking to one another in the nude made us more realistic about our physical selves. We took turns sharing how we felt about our bodies and our orgasms. I made it a point to go first to set an example by intimately sharing my own current feelings. It was amazing to hear a woman with a beautiful body tear herself apart, while another woman who was easily fifty pounds overweight explained she liked her body and felt comfortable in it. When a woman expressed unqualified love for her body, she became our inspiration for selflove.

When we talked about orgasm, our images were either unclear or confused. For one woman, the experience of orgasm was a major emotional event; for another, it was a minor pleasure, and for yet another, it was a complete mystery. Often one or two women weren't sure if they were having orgasms, and they either

had no idea what to expect or they had unrealistic romantic expectations. Several women who had said they were not coming discovered they were having little orgasms. They had thought all orgasms were shatteringly intense like the ones they had read about in erotic literature. Most of the other women were orgasmic one way or another, but they were interested in learning more about masturbation. Some women had good orgasms with oralsex but not with intercourse. Others could come with intercourse but couldn't get off alone. Still others were having orgasms with themselves but not with a partner. All of the orgasmic women agreed on one thing: their experience of orgasms varied greatly from one orgasm to the next.

After all the talking, it was time for action. I would start off by doing a skit imitating myself in the "proper" female role. I pretended to be teetering off balance in the modern footbinding of high heels. Draping myself into feminine poses, I occupied as small a space as possible. It was a good imitation because when I was a fashion illustrator, I'd taken "femininity" to its extremes. Everyone would laugh with recognition. Then we'd practice standing up straight, looking at our posture in a mirror. Walking tall with our heads up, tits out, buttocks tucked under, and clits forward completely changed our appearances and attitudes.

One amusing and informative exercise was called "Running a Sexual Encounter." It involved reversing sexroles with the women on top. We made believe that our clitorises were penetrating imaginary lovers, and we had to do all the thrusting. I would set the egg timer for three minutes, a little longer than Kinsey's national average. As the fucking began, I would participate and at the same time comment on everyone's technique. "Keep your arms straight; don't crush your lover. You're too high up; your clitoris just fell out. Don't stop moving; you'll lose your erection. Don't move so fast; you'll come too soon. And don't forget to whisper sweet things in your lover's ear between all those passionate kisses."

Watching the egg timer, I coordinated my theatrical orgasm with the ding of the bell, frantically thrusting for the last ten seconds. Then, falling flat on my imaginary lover, I muttered, "Was it good for you?" and promptly began snoring loudly. It was always hysterically funny.

Panting and exhausted, they all exclaimed, "How do men do it?" Complaints included tired arms, lower-back pain and stiff hip joints. Most of the women had fallen out long before the bell went off. After that, there was always more empathy for men, and the women showed an increased interest in other positions for lovemaking.

Some of the women talked about experiencing pain with deep-thrusting intercourse, while others claimed to want a hard fuck. In my youth, I'd confused hard pounding intercourse with passion, and experienced internal soreness afterward. I explained that I felt a sensitive lover would never thrust with violence. While I enjoyed a strong fuck when we were two equal energies in sync, I also loved the slow intense fuck.

Another problem the women complained of was lack of lubrication and the pain of dry intercourse. Some women felt inadequate if they weren't wet with passion. My experience varied; sometimes I lubricated when I wasn't even thinking about sex. Other times I could be dry even though I felt sexually aroused. I recommended using a massage oil to my group. Love oils and lubricants were always sensuous to me, and I never felt embarrassed about using one.

"Genital Show and Tell" was invariably a high point of every workshop. Of all the women in the groups I taught, I remember only a few who didn't participate during the "show" part. But everyone participated in the viewing as each woman's vaginal flower came into the spotlight. Seated before a makeup mirror, I always went first. Using both hands, I "split my bea-ver," exposing my cute little wattles while reminiscing about my past fears of genital deformity. After years of viewing women's genitals, I'd seen many inner lips much larger and longer than my own. I'd made such a big deal of my dangles that I felt like apologizing because they were so small.

Most women had a visual image of a penis, so I made an analogy between the clitoris and the penis. I pulled back the hood (foreskin) to expose the glans of the clitoris (glans of the penis), emphasizing the shaft of the clitoris (shaft of the penis) and explaining that both the ovaries and testicles were almond-shaped glands approximately the same size. Someone always said, "Oh, the clitoris is like a little penis," and I always answered, "Or a penis is like an oversized clitoris!"

During "Show and Tell," we reviewed our concerns about episiotomy scars from childbirth, inner lips that didn't match, little bumps or moles that looked strange, clitorises that were thought to be "too small," and the dreaded vaginal discharge. We talked about genital hygiene and how douching could be available but not as a compulsive routine.

Since most women have some clear or white secretion, I always considered that normal. I never used harsh commercial douching preparations, only white vinegar or plain water. Usu-ally washing the exterior genitalia and reaching just inside the vaginal opening was sufficient cleansing. Before making love, I inserted a finger inside my vagina to smell and taste myself, which made me feel secure. After I became a vegetarian, I noticed

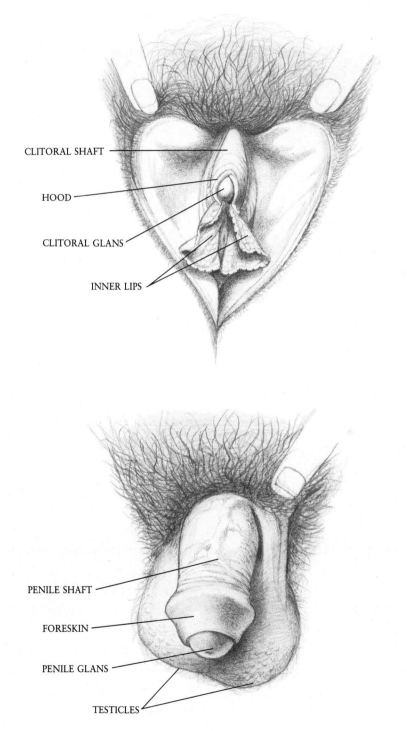

CLITORAL SHAFT

HOOD

CLITORAL GLANS

INNER LIPS

PENILE SHAFT

FORESKIN

PENILE GLANS

TESTICLES

that I tasted sweeter, and the same was true for my vegetarian lovers.

While each group was on the subject of genitals, we located the muscles of the vaginal barrel by inserting a finger in the vagina and squeezing. Most women understood "bearing down" from childbirth, or "pushing out" a bowel movement. This sex exercise was the opposite of bearing down. It was lifting up. Another way to locate the vaginal muscle was by stopping the flow of urine. Either way, tightening the muscle by pulling up and releasing produced pleasant genital sensations that grew stronger with practice. By pulling back the hood and watching in a mirror, some of us could also locate the separate muscle that moved the clitoris.

We also did anal selfmassage by oiling and gently pressing around the sphincter muscle before we inserted a finger. Breathing into the sensation, we further relaxed the muscles while letting go of any negative feelings about our assholes. Once relaxation occurred, pleasurable sensations followed. The poor anus is the last part of the body to get any loving, and I made it a point to call mine a "sweet little pink rosebud." Anal eroticism can become a beautiful part of sexual sharing.

When we discussed contraception, most of us agreed that each means had its problems. Most of the young women were on the pill. Personally, I felt the diaphragm was the safest, but it was a sophisticated form of birth control. I had to become sex positive before I was totally comfortable using one. Instead of jumping up in the middle of sex to insert it, my diaphragm always went in while I was showering, just before a date. It was also okay if I was wearing my diaphragm and sex didn't happen. At first I thought a diaphragm would spoil the spontaneity of the erotic moment, but I soon turned that around to feeling excited by the possibility of sex. A diaphragm inserter helped me to get it in place more easily. I always reached inside to check the correct positioning, and then washed off the excess spermicidal jelly outside and inside my vagina. After I wore it for an hour or so the natural taste and smell of my cunt returned. When I became skilled, the whole procedure took only a few minutes. Later I discovered that the Nonoxynol-9 in my spermicidal jelly helped protect me from VD. Laboratory tests have also proved that Nonoxynol-9 kills the AIDS virus, and it can be found in some brands of condoms. Nowadays smart women are carrying condoms in their purses to ensure casual safesex.

Many of the Bodysex women experienced their first massage in the groups. They were always turned on by the sensuality and relaxation. We divided up into two groups. In each, one woman at a time would lie down and be massaged by the other five or six women in her group. The circle of massagers would rotate with each turn so that everyone touched different parts of the body. It was a visual delight to see one woman in the center of a circle, receiving the energy from a dozen loving hands touching her all at the same time. An orgy of sensation! Everyone had the chance both to give and receive pleasure, enjoying all kinds of delicious sensations without having to respond sexually. Women as well as men suffer from "performance anxieties," and massage gives us all the opportunity to be "off stage"—to simply let go, stop thinking, and just feel. For couples who have been together many years, I always recommend the combination of massage and masturbation. Instead of programmed foreplay and the same sex position, this kind of erotic sharing can open up new experiences in intimacy without pressure.

In one of the early groups we had been talking about the absence of erotic games for little girls. I shared my fantasy of some day having a women's "circle jerk." "That sounds like fun. Let's do it now," several women said. It blew my mind! They were ready for group masturbation, but *I* wasn't. For me it was still a fantasy. I was on the edge of freaking out, until I reassured myself that we were all consenting adults and joined in. Placing an orange candle in the center of the circle, I lit it with a trembling hand. A shiver ran up my spine. Had I once been an Egyptian priestess? Suddenly my inner voice said, "This is an ancient Tantra ritual and you are under divine guidance."

In the beginning, "Circle Masturbation" was optional in each group. By the fifth year, it evolved into the "Guided Masturbation Ritual" and became a part of every group. We began by standing in a circle, dancing to music with our vibrators, an exotic vision of female erotica. I guided the group through different kinds of genital stimulation, pelvic movements, breathing patterns, and sexual positions for masturbating. One of my favorites was getting on top of our vibrators, which we placed on pillows. It was the best position for practicing pelvic thrusting. We went on to other variations that emphasized different leg positions.

After about thirty minutes, I declared an erotic recess. The energy would bounce off the walls along with sexual sighs of pleasure. The women loved the ritual with or without an orgasm, sensing that it was moving us through a lifetime of sexual repression in one hour! We were bringing masturbation out of the nuclear family's darkest closet and putting selfsexuality into the Temple of Pleasure.

The Bodysex Groups took me on inner trips of agony and ecstasy. I constantly worried about going too far, struggling with the concept that women were conservative and timid about taking risks. But that turned out not to be true. Every woman who entered the Temple was a powerhouse of courage even though she might have been resistant about undressing. Sometimes I felt like I was wading through a swamp of repression, up to my knees in inhibitions. I had to absorb the group's resistance and then release the tension through the pleasure rituals. The ecstasy came when I looked around the circle of masturbating women and nearly swooned from the erotic image.

I know there have been many parties or neighborhood coffee klatches where a Bodysex woman captured her listeners with a description of her sexual adventure. The women also told their husbands and lovers about their experiences in detail, and that opened up sexual communications, often for the first time. Educators, therapists, and healers took my masturbation information into their own work with other people. Every Bodysex Group dropped a pebble into the pond of repression. The radiating rings of sexual energy spread far and wide, touching the lives of many women and men with erotic love.

The groups were my teacher as I taught sex by doing sex. Once I estimated I had guided over five thousand women through orgasm rituals. These women were all my divine lovers. It will always be impossible to describe the magnificent visuals or to touch the depths of the emotional and sexual content. The Bodysex Groups never ceased to fill me with respect for the power and beauty of sexual energy.

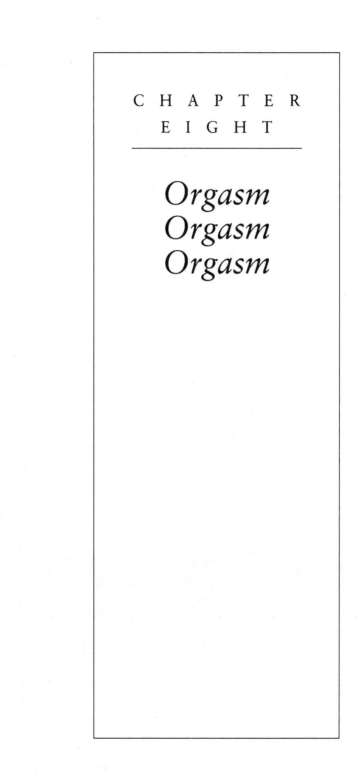

CHAPTER EIGHT

Orgasm Orgasm Orgasm

Whether it comes from a lover, a bathtub, a teddy bear, a dildo, a finger, a tongue, or a vibrator, an orgasm is an orgasm is an orgasm. My adult orgasm rituals of selfloving were quite modest in the beginning. It took about ten minutes for me to come, and then I stopped. I used sensate focus, which meant I paid attention only to my body's sensations. Gradually I started taking more time and being a better lover for myself. I began coming up more slowly, dropping back, and teasing myself, building up more sexual tension before letting go. When I started to focus my mind with erotic thoughts and images, orgasms got even better. To develop a sexual fantasy life, I would first mentally review a good sexual experience. Reading sex books, looking at sexual art, and finding porn that turned me on also inspired me to play with new fantasies.

I did the classical hand job, dipping a finger into my vagina for wetness. Sometimes I would hold my finger inside while I stimulated my clitoris with my other hand. It was always a pleasing sensation. One night I watched myself masturbating with the magnifying side of a makeup mirror. It was a fabulous sight, like watching an erotic movie on a miniature screen. I added style to the way I handled myself. I could see my vaginal lips change to a deeper red, and my clitoris got bigger with sexual arousal. Doing an internal vaginal massage with three fingers increased lubrication, and my sexual juices glistened in the light. I ended up moving my hand so rapidly it was a blur just before I came. When I had my orgasm, the curtain of my eyelids ended the movie.

At first, I never had more than one orgasm when I masturbated. My clitoris was always too sensitive to touch immediately after coming. One Sunday afternoon I carved a white candle into a lovely penis-shaped dildo and held it inside while I diddled my clit. After having a "meaningful" orgasm, I was still turned on but too sensitive to go again. Suddenly I flashed on the idea of breathing the way women are taught in natural childbirth classes to help them cope with pain. I began doing the same panting breath to cope with more pleasure, and discovered I could continue with a lighter touch. Within moments, the hypersensitivity disappeared, and I was into another sexual buildup. Instead of holding my breath and pulling back, from then on I increased my breathing to match the strong sensation. I moved through what I'd once labeled "pain" into a new experience with pleasure.

After that I began an exercise that taught me a lot about tolerating higher levels of body sensations. After taking a hot tub or sauna, I started jumping into cold water. At first the thought of doing it was terrible, often nearly paralyzing. I had usually avoided both extreme heat or cold since they were such intense

sensations. But the reality of the experience was also exhilarating, stimulating to my circulation and senses. *The space between the thought and the action was inhibition.* My ability to move through that space was relative to my willingness to seek new pleasures.

Jumping into pleasure got easier for me. In the late sixties, I had my first vibrator orgasm from an electric scalp massager that belonged to Blake. It looked like a little cement mixer trimmed with chrome that was held onto the back of the hand with two bands of coiled metal springs. One night he offered to give me a massage and started with my head. It felt wonderful. As he slowly moved his hand down my body, my heart beat faster. I jumped when his vibrating fingers began dancing rapidly over my clitoris. The pleasure was so intense that I grabbed his arm. When he asked if I wanted him to stop, I wisely said no. I breathed into the sensation, and after my third thrilling orgasm, I was into another kind of intensity.

Then I bought an electric scalp massager that came neatly packed in a box surrounded by a group of strange little rubber attachments. I selected a suction cup, snapped it into place, and plugged in the vibrator. Catching my breath, I realized that, though nearly silent, it was very intense. By putting my finger over my clitoris with the rim of the cup vibrating my finger, I began panting and managed to have a fast come. But when I wanted to continue, the machine heated up, and it was no fun playing with a toy that was too hot to handle.

In the early seventies, a new electric body massager hit the market. It was a big, awesome, cylindrical machine that sounded like a truck in low gear. The handle was nine inches long, and it had a three-inch rubber head. Everyone I showed it to nearly swooned until I explained that it wasn't used for penetration. All that heavy equipment was meant to vibrate my sweet little clitoris. It was the beginning of my love affair with a machine that I fondly called "Big Mack." (My friend immediately got one and named hers "Lucky Pierre.")

At first I used my new massage machine mostly on my neck and shoulders, following the instructions. It took a while to figure out how to harness all that energy for sexual pleasure. One night, Big Mack and I sneaked up on my clitoris, which was under a towel that was folded over at least three times. Just as I feared—instant ecstasy! I was overwhelmed with pleasure anxiety. This machine could even be turned from low to high. I was now capable of dialing these incredible orgasms, and Mack was good for hours without getting too hot.

In retrospect, I can see there were times I came close to romantic love with my vibrator. I solved the problem of possessiveness by buying several and lending them to friends. I later ended up buying them by the case for my Bodysex Groups, until one day I discovered Big Mack was no longer being manufactured. I thought the government had moved in to curtail our orgasms, but the Goddess provides, and another electric body massager appeared. It was slender and more graceful, with a motor that purred like a big cat.

Whenever I came home, there was my new electric vibrator, "Pandora," waiting faithfully to give me endless hours of pleasure. She never had a headache or was too tired to please me, and she never complained when I was into "people sex." What saved me from going steady was careful consideration of Pandora's shortcomings: all buzz and no conversation, and she never initiated lovemaking. But I was able to love my vibrator for itself, a delightful toy that provided good vibrations.

Since I continued to have orgasmic sex with my lovers, I finally stopped being afraid of becoming vibrator addicted. I also stopped worrying about wearing my clitoris down to a nub or becoming antisocial. None of that happened. I was far more antisocial when I was love addicted. In those days, what began as pleasure quickly turned into pain as I became obsessed with my beloved. I've never been obsessed with a vibrator. My experience with addictions has taught me that pain and frustration induce a fixation. I was like the mice in the scientist's maze: those conditioned with pain remained on the same course, while those conditioned with pleasure roamed off onto new paths.

Until the end of the seventies, my masturbation rituals usually involved a vibrator only. Then I began experimenting again with penetration. I oiled a silicone dildo and put it at the entrance of my vagina while I used the vibrator on my clitoris. Doing slow, sensuous penetration, I moved on it, tightening and releasing my vaginal muscles. Just before I came, I held the dildo inside by squeezing my legs together. Both hands were on the vibrator while I tensed my buttocks and picked up the beat.

I love the happy little orgasms I get from a fifteen-minute sex break. They energize my body and discharge accumulated tension. At the other end of the scale are the several delicious orgasms that end a two-hour ritual. Building up, counting down, and dancing on the edge for as long as possible, I use every body movement, breathing pattern, and erotic thought in my repertoire. It's a total commitment to hedonism. I've laughed, cried, and moaned going for the big one. After I have had three or more orgasms, I'm so high I just stay there, breathing and riding the waves of pleasure. I continue vibrating and trembling, no longer interested in coming because I'm beyond orgasm and into a state of ecstasy that can last up to ten minutes. Tapering off with lesser spasms, I finally sink back to earth after a cosmic flight.

Getting into the high-powered thrills electric vibration can give is an individual choice. I love electric orgasms, but some women prefer the penis-shaped battery-operated vibrators, and that's fine. Vibrators are so perfect for orgasms that it's easy to forget how wonderful they are for massage. Whenever you vibrate, you are stimulating the flow of blood to that area, a marvelous health and beauty treatment for the entire body. It's important to remember that, with any electrical appliance, *you must keep your vibrator away from water.*

When a woman is new to vibrator sex, she may experience any number of responses. One friend reported that the first time she used her vibrator, she had the most intense orgasm of her life, but it was over before she knew what had happened. Another said her orgasm was ever so slight, lasting only a second. And yet another woman had to practice patiently for several months before anything sexual happened. Little orgasms that occur within moments of contact are similar to men's premature ejaculations. Masturbating is the best way in the world to learn to control the urge to come quickly for both men and women. By loving those little quick comes, your orgasms will grow longer and stronger.

I have friends who prefer indirect stimulation. They have orgasms by pressure alone, pressing their thighs together and tensing their muscles rhythmically. I know a young man who presses his penis against the bed to masturbate. As a child, I used the pressure technique with a pillow between my legs, but now I want more direct contact. Other women prefer water stimulation and enjoy orgasms in the bathtub with a shower massager. One friend of mine accidentally had an orgasm in the whirlpool at her health club by sitting in front of a jet stream. An orgasm is an orgasm is an orgasm.

There are many women who can't learn how to have a first orgasm with pressure, water, or manual masturbation. If a woman has had little or no experience with childhood or adult masturbation, she has learned to say no to sexual feelings. For these women an electric vibrator provides strong, steady stimulation that can make up for the years of sensory deprivation. It may be the only way she can achieve orgasm for months or years, but that isn't nearly as devastating as *never* experiencing an orgasm. Electric orgasms can be as fulfilling as any other kind.

In our desire to be "good girls and boys," we can literally cut off the feelings in our sex organs. Extreme repression can block the pathways of the nervous system that carry genital sensations to the brain. Wilhelm Reich, the well-known psychoanalyst who wrote *The Function of the Orgasm*, described orgasm as ". . . the ability to surrender to the flow of sexual energy *without any inhibition;* the capacity for complete discharge of all sexual excitation through involuntary pleasurable contractions of the whole body." It is a wonderful description, but for years it didn't apply to me. Like many people, I'd been unable to experience orgasm fully.

Until my mid-thirties, my poor body had been racked with pain from hangovers, chronic muscle tension, lack of exercise, and bad nutrition—all of which interfered with erotic sensations. Mind inhibitors were guilt, fear, anger, and self-pity, which deprived me of erotic thoughts. These classical body/mind blocks impeded the flow of my sex energy, discharging it in my gentials only. I only had little orgasms that were like hiccups.

All my years of childhood and marital masturbation were about *not getting caught*. I'd trained myself to come fast while remaining silent. When I was with a lover, I avoided heavy breathing, barely moved my body, and never broke out in a sweat. In order to have "ladylike orgasms," I always held back because, basically, I was embarrassed about sex.

A married woman in one of my Bodysex Workshops told me how she reached her first orgasm at age forty-eight. One night she put her new vibrator on her clitoris and two hours later she exploded into an orgasm that nearly threw her off the bed, and she weighed almost two hundred pounds! The vibrator was the consistent stimulation her body wanted. Neither she nor her husband ever had the stamina to hang in there long enough. Now they are thrilled with their new sexlife: intercourse is foreplay for her, and after he comes, she has a vibrator orgasm while they kiss and hug. They are having a sexual honeymoon.

Another Bodysex woman was feeling desperate after ten years of marriage, one child, and no orgasms. She finally got a vibrator and put it directly on her genitals for a long time, several nights in a row, determined to experience pleasure. The vibrator made her sore for a few days. Lacking genital feelings, she'd accidentally created pain instead of pleasure. She was furious! But at least the pain had proved to her that there was life "down there," and she didn't give up. With more practice and a lighter

touch, she started getting pleasurable sensations.

A lesbian friend learned how to have her first orgasms with a vibrator in her mid-thirties. Within a year she was also able to have orgasms with her lover through oralsex. Five years later she was thrilled when she learned how to masturbate by hand. She said she felt more complete knowing she was no longer dependent upon a machine or a person. Now she could create her own orgasms. Making the transition from the vibrator to her hand had been impossible until she began using sexual fantasies. When she was with her lover, she thought about her, and when she used her vibrator she thought about nothing. Now when she masturbates by hand, she thinks about sex. To turn herself on without a vibrator or a lover, she needed to use her mind.

One thirty-two-year-old woman I knew had spent ten years coming only with a vibrator. When she finally met the man she was to marry, she wanted to learn how to have an orgasm during lovemaking. She began by changing her masturbation pattern, putting her hand between the vibrator and her clitoris. Gradually, she learned how to respond to a lighter touch. At the end of six months she had trained herself to come by hand, and it was no problem for her to have an orgasm during intercourse with her husband's hand stimulating her clitoris.

A bisexual friend who'd been using a vibrator in between lovers decided to give it away. She said her electric orgasms were so easy that she stopped having sexual fantasies. She went back to getting off by hand while sitting in a warm bath reading hot porn. Several years later, she got another vibrator, realizing she could use it, still have her fantasies, and go for more than one orgasm, even when she had a lover.

Sexual fantasy can be full of paradox. A married woman I knew was worried because her fantasies were primarily about women, although she considered herself to be completely heterosexual. A lesbian friend of mine wondered why she often had heterosexual fantasies, when in reality she never felt turned on by men. It's a shame that we walk through life with sexual labels between our legs. As long as we identify ourselves as heterosexual, bisexual, homosexual, instead of just plain "sexual," the friends of sex remain divided against one another. The moralistic minority speaks out while the sexual majority remains silent. It's time for us to support sexual pleasure in whatever form it takes to get on with life, liberty, and the pursuit of happiness. An orgasm is an orgasm is an orgasm.

A friend who considered herself a radical feminist got concerned that her sexual imagery wasn't politically correct because it wasn't "feminist oriented." I assure her that all fantasies were okay. Lots of people imagine scenes they never want to experience. I also pointed out that we can become addicted to a fantasy like anything else, and suggested she experiment with new ones. One of her new assertive fantasies is about moving her clitoris in and out of her lover's soft wet mouth while he's tied down. Whenever she gets stuck or is in a hurry, she brings out her old fantasy of being raped by five Irish cops and always reaches orgasm quickly.

Fantasies about rape can turn us on in our minds because we're masturbating with pleasurable sensations in our bodies. For me, there's no such thing as "feminist fantasies" or "feminist sex." Women's liberation isn't about defining politically correct sex; it's about exploring and increasing our erotic potential. I can support feminists who want the ideal of "perfect love between equals" in a monogamous relationship that will last "forever." By the same token, I want them to support my ideal of living with an erotic family of friends. There will never be one "right way" to have fantasies and orgasms.

In the beginning of my love affair with women's liberation, I was like any romantic lover: I idealized "all women." I thought feminists were the chosen few who would lead the world out of the mess it was in. Until the new erotic images unfolded, we were like an army talking about the "front lines," "the enemy," and winning "the battle between the sexes." No joy there!

Eventually I learned that feminists weren't perfect, and life wasn't fair. Sexual revolutions wax and wane. Only personal histories of evolution are consistent. By eroticizing our own lives, we become inspirations for others. Instead of being women *against* pornography, we are women *for* sexual expression, new erotic images, and we are willing to evolve sex and pleasure into art. It's time to replace radical feminism with erotic feminism as we move along new paths of personal liberation.

I believe the ability to fantasize, visualize, or dream is at the heart of my creative process. Fantasy is a way of playing with my mind and developing my imagination. My erotic art, the Bodysex Groups, and this book all began as sexual fantasies.

One of my recent sexual fantasies is about power. Dressed in black leather with a diamond-studded chain belt, I'm standing at the head of a large conference table in an elegant wood-paneled boardroom. Addressing the executive officers of all the multinational corporations, I outline my proposal to eroticize the corporate structure by bringing orgasms to business. They're spellbound as I project architectural drawings of the new executive lounges

97

that are filled with elaborate sexual equipment that guarantees ecstasy. It's unanimously agreed to put pleasure before profit, and now that sexual energy is in, all the nuclear plants can be shut down.

Bodysex for Men

Over the years, I kept getting requests from men who wanted to do a Bodysex Group because their lovers or wives had taken one. At first, I simply said no to the prospect. But the more I thought about it, the more intriguing it became. The idea of a woman teaching· a group of men how to masturbate was an outrageous role reversal, and, being a sucker for a challenge, one day I took a deep breath, threw my shoulders back, and said, "Why not?"

My first men's group appeared to be made up of heterosexual men, so it would have been easy to focus on teaching them about female sexuality. But I was committed to getting them to explore their own sexuality through masturbation. They were gentle men, not at all macho, and the mix of professions was interesting: three sex educators, two ministers, an artist, a young graduate student, and three businessmen.

On the first day, after a few hours of intellectual discussion, I badgered them into talking about their sexual fears, urging them to speak in the first person, which they never did. Concern about sexual performance emerged as their major sex problem. The men worried about coming too quickly or not getting erections. For women, performance anxiety took the form of not feeling sexy, not lubricating, or not having an orgasm. While I listened to these men, I realized that the quality of their own orgasms seemed relatively unimportant. They were mainly focused on giving their women sexual pleasure and orgasms, rating their "good lover" image by their partner's responses. Women might fear sex, but men feared sexual failure.

The "Genital Show and Tell" ritual fizzled and died because they said a penis wasn't a mystery; they saw their genitals every day. I couldn't get a discussion going about penis size, nor could I provoke any personal comments on their relationship with their cocks. Did a man think his cock was appealing? Did he think it was pretty? Did he like the way his penis felt when he masturbated? Not much response. They weren't interested in looking at each other's genitals because they saw them all the time in the locker rooms and at urinals.

Show and Tell ended when I revved up my courage and did my first live "split beaver" for a group of men. I was amazed that they were so shy about looking, which only made me bolder. I wound up wiggling my clit with abandon and for a finale, demonstrating cunt breathing—forcing air in and out of my vaginal opening. It usually brought a round of applause from women, but the men seemed overawed by the idea of a *muscular vagina*.

That night I couldn't get to sleep because I was so worried. How was I going to conduct a guided masturbation ritual the next day? After years of emphasizing the similarities between men and women, I was now overwhelmed by our differences. I lay there trying to imagine what it would feel like to have a cock and balls. Looking down, I fantasized my clit sticking out seven inches from my body. Every time I went to the bathroom, I'd be taking hold of my clitoris. Was urinating a constant reminder of sex? And what would it feel like to wake up with a hard-on? With a sex organ that big, maybe just getting hard and ejaculating was pleasure enough, and that's why men weren't so concerned with the quality of their orgasms. Watching my seven-inch clit shoot sperm would surely be a thrill, even without a "total body orgasm."

For a moment I got a rush of penis envy, something I vowed didn't exist. Though I was still cunt positive and loved my little clitoris, walking around with exterior gentials had to make male sexuality a lot different from female sexuality. Imagine! I was thirty-five years old before I had a positive image of my own genitals. Men hauled out their dicks several times a day just to pee. Whatever possessed me to run a masturbation workshop for men in the first place?

On the second day, one of the men brought me a cute rubber penis. It was as though he'd read my mind from last night and wanted to help. I actually blushed, thanked him, and put the pink dildo next to my electric vibrator, which was much larger. I liked these thoughtful men. They genuinely wanted to learn, and I had a feeling they were rooting for me. But again the discussion got very intellectual—they kept talking about how men feared fear without naming anything specific or personal. I was sitting there just as frozen as they were. I had to act.

Sounding like a general ordering her troops to the front lines of pleasure, I announced it was time for the masturbation ritual. Jumping to my feet, I plugged in my vibrator and watched all my men stretch out on the floor carefully so as not to touch the man on either side. As they tentatively touched their limp penises, their bodies were as stiff as boards. Not one of them was breathing.

Standing there ready to perform, I saw they all had their eyes closed. I reminded them they were paying me to demonstrate masturbation, but no one was looking at me. When all eyes were finally open and focused on me, the intensity almost threw me off balance. I started making eye contact with one man at a time, doing a kind of visual serial monogamy until I got centered again. I encouraged each man to breathe, move his pelvis, use plenty of oil on his penis and glance around the group to get the visuals and be inspired by the others.

My wide-angle view of the whole scene brought a hot sexual rush and a surge of power. There I was, a small woman, towering over ten large naked men, masturbating at my feet!

One of the therapists, a man I'd known for several years, looked at me squarely with sex sparks in his eyes. Roger was a giant of a man, a patriarch with gray hair and full white beard. He resembled God in Michelangelo's painting of the Creation except for his big, dark-brown genitals. He was gracefully stroking the length of his cock, which was nearly as long as my twelve-inch vibrator. I started to match his pelvic movements, stroking the length of my clitoris.

When Roger came, it was loud and long, a real force. His orgasm had a domino effect. First Dick, next John, and then Rick came. My legs started trembling, and I sank to the floor. Hank, on my left, abandoned his own pleasure to watch mine. Bobby, the artist, was on my right, and when my foot touched his, the heat ignited both of us. We let out primeval howls as we had simultaneous orgasms.

The group cheered. I sat up, hugged the men on either side of me, and said I wanted a hug from each man. Everyone stood up and started embracing everyone else. What a sight it was! A whole roomful of naked heterosexual men, hugging each other like big bears, not A-frame hugs but full body hugs with love and acceptance.

When we sat in the circle to talk, John, the minister, thought the experience was "uplifting," that my sexual warmth had been contagious. Rick was amazed by the difference between his childhood circle jerks and our masturbation ritual, where the objective was communal acceptance of selflove. He felt he'd never been able to caress his own body tenderly because he'd been afraid to like his own maleness. Roger pointed out that men usually countered their fear of liking men with anger and aggression. Sharing orgasms and naked hugs was a radical break from social conditioning. Hank, the only one who didn't have an orgasm, said watching me was an inspiration to practice loving himself. "We'll all be better lovers by loving ourselves more," I answered.

There weren't any spontaneous group hugs in my next several groups, but I included a group massage ritual that always got the men touching each other. It was even a bigger thrill for me to watch men doing massage together than women. Somehow it seemed more natural to see women touching and nurturing one another. Being with a group of nude husbands and fathers massaging each other made me nearly weep with joy. There was an esprit de corps from the gentle laying on of hands.

Working with men in the Bodysex Groups was a good way for me to confront my own stereotypes about the opposite sex. For example, in one group we did some martial arts warm-up exercises. I showed the men the "horse" posture, standing with legs apart and knees bent, and had them punching out with fists from the waist. I was flabbergasted to see that a third of the group couldn't do it. My stupid assumption that all men knew how to punch got blasted away. Still I loved doing the more physical things with them because they were conditioned to push beyond their limits. Women usually stopped the minute they felt any exertion, but men went beyond where they were comfortable. They inspired me to push my own limits.

One of my breakthroughs was allowing myself to act like a Marine sergeant. Men knew how to take orders. When I became a no-nonsense disciplinarian, they loved it. I'd grown accustomed to never giving a women's group a direct order because most women reacted to being pushed by going right into passive resistance. I didn't have to baby men by making suggestions or easing them into the next activity. I simply stated what I wanted them to do, and they did it. Men had learned a different set of rules through team sports, the military, and the corporate structure.

Though I secretly felt I deserved an honorary degree for teaching masturbation, I was often treated socially like the latest dirty joke. Laughing about sex is a way for people to release their embarrassment, so I always laughed with them. But there were also times when I knew my work was appreciated. When I ran a group for sex educators, they gave me a lot of credit. A therapist who was writing about male masturbation said I was "an innovator who'd established a solid reputation in the field of masturbation." I laughed and said it was an honor from which I tried to resign each year. When these credentialed men all agreed that my groups had constituted "remarkable fieldwork," I thanked them. I knew that was one of the highest compliments academia could give.

This group got a good discussion going about circumcision. Several MDs said it was important for cleanliness, but one of the Ph.D.s insisted it was wrong to do it as a hospital routine because he thought the removal of the foreskin desensitized the penis. Half of the group agreed with him, and the other half thought just the opposite, that circumcision sensitized the penis. I was thrilled to have some feelings being expressed about a subject that rarely got discussed. I thought the pain of circumcision had to leave its mark on a baby boy. I added that, if I had a son, his penis would be left intact.

Several men spoke of teaching themselves how to control the urge to ejaculate with masturbation so they could prolong intercourse. It was basically the old Masters and Johnson squeeze technique. When they felt ejaculation approaching, they pressed thumb and forefinger together just under the head of their cocks, tightened anal muscles, and did deep breathing. Their erection partially subsided until they brought it back with more stimulation.

One man in his fifties had gone to an extreme, learning to hold off so long that he couldn't come when he wanted to. Two hours of fucking would often end with no orgasm for him. He said he envied younger men who could have fast, strong orgasms, while they envied his control.

Two of the older men talked about not being able to orgasm anymore from regular intercourse because they didn't get enough stimulation from a vagina. One of these men was married to a woman who'd taken a Bodysex Group, and they had agreed on a new erotic design: fancy fucking for fun, and then when they wanted to have their orgasms, they masturbated together. Once they let go of the idea that there was a "right" way to have sex, they had orgasms in abundance.

Most of the men in my groups believed in the thirty-minute refractory period so they automatically stopped masturbating after they came. But a few men had learned how to become multiorgasmic. One man, Sergio, talked about training himself to come more than once. First he had to be really turned on mentally. Then, by using a martial-arts breathing pattern, he could come, keep his erection, and go on fucking or masturbating through two more full-body orgasms. He said his semen diminished with each successive orgasm. When I asked Sergio if an orgasm with a full ejaculation was better than one without, he grinned and said, "They're all great!"

Very few of the guys were interested in trying a vibrator, which I couldn't understand, so sometimes I got a bit pushy. In one group, an older man, Al, had come within the first five minutes and then stopped masturbating. I got up and went over to him. Picking up an electric vibrator, I put it in his hands, turned on the switch, and guided it over his limp penis until I saw a faint smile on his lips. Later Al told the group how amazed he was to have had a second orgasm with a vibrator and a soft-on.

My last few men's groups got a surprise on their second day when I opened the door nude, wearing only a pink plastic dildo that was at least nine inches long. It caused a lot of hilarity. As I bragged about having the biggest dick, invariably someone would say "It's what you do with what you got." Several years after I stopped doing men's groups, I ran into one of my Bodysex men at a party. After Claude and I had hugged, he asked, "Do you still have your six-shooter?" When I didn't understand, he answered by turning to his friend and telling her the story about my opening the door wearing nothing but a "gun." I told him I didn't own a gun, but in Claude's memory, the nine-inch dildo had turned into a six-shooter.

One of the last workshops was particularly successful, and I was sure it was because there was an equal mix of heterosexual, bisexual, and gay men, which brought about a lot of enlightening dialogue. It was 1981, just before AIDS was to cast a pall over the gay men's community.

Most of the heterosexual men said they believed in monogamy, but during the discussion that followed, I discovered that none of them practiced it full time. When I asked how they would feel if their lovers and wives fooled around occasionally, only one man thought it would be fine. For him, monogamy or "faithfulness" was for insecure people. It had nothing to do with love. One of the gay men, George, thought monogamy was never meant for men; it was for the protection of women. I told him I thought it protected men. A monogamous wife not only ensured the paternity of her children, but also had no chance to make sexual comparisons, which protected her husband from any feelings of inadequacy. Michael said that while being gay meant a single sexual standard, sexual competition was out of control for homosexuals. A gay man had to be youthful, gorgeous, well built, and well hung. I laughed, reminding him that heterosexual women knew all about that. Michael said he wanted to be a lesbian in his next life.

Phillip, a bisexual man, said he couldn't imagine having to choose between being gay or straight. But our homophobic society made it difficult for a man to be openly bisexual. He said he was hesitant to talk about his homosexual experiences in front of straight men because it diminished his masculine image. He felt bisexuality didn't detract from a woman's feminine image. On the contrary, it could enhance her desirability. Watching two

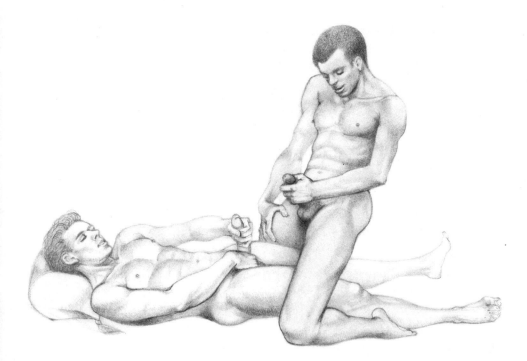

women making love was many heterosexual men's favorite fantasy. He couldn't imagine one of his women lovers ever wanting
to watch him get it on with a man or one of his gay lovers
watching him with a woman. I told Phillip we were now going to
watch each other.

When I passed out the bottles of almond massage oil and
paper towels, I pointed out the vibrators that were plugged in
around the room. "I want all of you to try a vibrator for at least
five minutes so you can see what they're like. I don't want the
electronic age of sex to pass you by," I said.

The circle masturbation became very erotic. I saw some
first-rate hand jobs going down. There were long, sensuous,
milking strokes, delicate tip tickling, double-handed twists, and
the usual rapid up and down beats on glistening hard cocks. I
saw several men holding their testicles with one hand while they

masturbated with the other. Then I closed my eyes and went within to concentrate on the good feeling in my clitoris. Another vibrator besides mine was humming. At one point, I heard several orgasms swell up around the circle and that's when I came. I looked up just in time to see George, the last cock in action, spurting jism on his belly as he groaned out loud. Most of the men came on themselves and then wiped up the little puddle of sperm with the paper towels. Ejaculations didn't fly all over the room as some of my women friends imagined when they asked me about the men's groups. Women showed as much curiosity as men, and I got lots of requests to install a two-way mirror for voyeurs. That was a hot fantasy for both sexes.

The sharing afterward was moving. Several straight men said the best thing about the group had been getting over their fear of gay men. One gay man, Allan, said he was in the gay world most of the time, so it was wonderful to get in touch with men who were husbands and fathers. Gerald, who never identified his sexstyle, said, "It's too bad that straight and gay men never get to interact. It leaves everyone with fixed ideas that aren't true." When Peter complained about having to live in the gay ghetto, John said he'd spent all of his life in the middle-class-married ghetto. Everyone agreed that listening to each other talk openly about his sexlife made them all real people instead of superficial sexlabels.

Although I ran only a dozen men's groups, the experience helped me to let go of my old conviction that men got a better deal when it came to sex. My habit of thinking in clichés and making sweeping assumptions had me believing that male socialization gave all men more sexual freedom. I thought they could always have easy orgasms even with casual sex, and I envied their never having to worry about the biological realities of periods or pregnancies. But the truth is that not all men are able to be assertive studs who make out all the time. Many men in the groups were shy and insecure, especially when it came to partnersex. It was true that some teenagers or immature men don't give a damn about getting a woman pregnant, but I learned there are also men who feel a lot of responsibility about birth control. I also discovered those easy orgasms are frequently premature ejaculations, little hiccups that aren't very satisfying. Researchers never got around to acknowledging the existence of preorgasmic men. And the most consistent sex problem for many men in the workshops was owning a penis that seemed to have a will of its own. An unpredictable sex organ that got hard when no one was around and then refused to erect when a man was holding the woman of his dreams in his arms.

More than anything else, my work with men made me very aware that men and women still had a lot to learn about one another. It would be wonderful if we could put ourselves in each other's shoes to see how it feels. Empathy and compassion will eventually heal all those ancient resentments between the sexes. I hereby forgive all the men in my life who didn't turn out to be what I expected, and I also forgive myself for having had all those romantic expectations. No one, no place, nothing is perfect. That's a tough lesson, one I keep learning in order to love life more fully.

Masturbation as Meditation

When I wrote, illustrated, and published my first book under the title *Liberating Masturbation*, it was a do-it-yourself tour de force. Just minutes before the manuscript went to the typesetters, I got a flash of inspiration and added a subtitle: *A Meditation on Selflove*. Somehow the words *masturbation* and *meditation* looked right together, and I loved the way they sounded. But then I found myself in the embarrassing position of not being able to explain *why* masturbation was a form of meditation. Intuitively I knew it was true, though I had no actual evidence.

The following year, I started practicing TM—Transcendental Meditation. Twice a day, I sat quietly for twenty minutes repeating my mantra, and I did feel more peaceful. But then I got into a busy spell, and my meditation became sporadic. One night when I was masturbating, I got the wonderful idea of repeating my mantra at the same time. It added a spiritual dimension to my sexual selfloving. Instead of two twenty-minute sessions a day, I started doing one forty-minute meditation at night with my vibrator, repeating my mantra and ending with an orgasm. I was practicing Transcendental Masturbation.

It was clear that masturbation as a ritual created harmony

between my body and mind the same way that meditation did. After having an orgasm, or after meditating, I was always more peaceful, centered in my body, and relaxed in my mind. Once I realized that masturbation was an active form of meditation, I thought, Hallelujah! Now everyone will want to meditate.

When I told my meditating friends about my discovery, they were shocked by the association and acted as though it were akin to blasphemy. My obsession with sex had finally led me to irreverence. My erotic friends laughed and thought the combination of the two activities was humorous. A few patted me on the head with understanding tolerance, assuming I wanted to aggrandize masturbation. So it was just another one of my sexual hallucinations. No one was interested. The spiritual community wanted to sublimate their sexual energy, while the sexual community just wanted to enjoy it without being burdened by esoteric ritual. I finally stopped using my mantra for masturbation and quietly, without protest, went back to variations on my old whorehouse fantasy.

Then I finally got scientific data to back up my radical erotic concept. My friend Raymond, a Ph.D. sex researcher, was conducting a project at the medical school of Rutgers University to demonstrate the significance of brain phenomena during orgasm. He was investigating how sexual behavior affects the right and left brain hemispheres, something I knew nothing about. He would be monitoring brain activity with an electroencephalograph (EEG) while also recording cardiac, circulatory, and muscular changes in the body. Raymond thought I would be an ideal subject, and I thought it would be a pleasure to jerk off for science and the national data bank. I was also excited by the idea of getting all this physiological information about my body and brain.

On the appointed day, I arrived at Rutgers with a quart of fresh carrot juice circulating through my body. Volunteers were requested to be drug-free. I'd also been instructed to bring my trusty electric vibrator plus a record of my choice. I picked the

Allman Brothers to be my musical lovers with their *Eat a Peach* album. The room was softly lit with incense burning to eliminate any clinical atmosphere. I felt right at home with all my accoutrements.

My foreplay consisted of two beautiful nurses sensitively taping wires to my head, my chest, my vagina, and finally even my toes. Taking their time, they made sure I was comfortable before they left me alone. The space was totally private. Only an intercom connected my room to a laboratory that had all the most sophisticated scientific equipment available. My sexual buildup and orgasm were going to be measured by three highly skilled technicians whom I would never see. The whole scene already had me lubricating.

My sexual fantasy was visualizing that reality. I imagined my three faceless lovers in white coats, fingering dials and carefully adjusting instruments as they watched the readout on Anonymous Subject Number 5503. I had a medium-sized orgasm toward the end of the record, at which point my favorite drum solo filled the room. Shifting gears, I went into breath-of-fire yoga breathing, threw the vibrator switch to high, and pulled up alongside my steady drummer. We were both heading for a really big orgasm.

Just one moment away from ecstasy, my drummer was abruptly cut off. I gasped. A cool, impersonal voice came from the intercom: "Thank you. That will be all. You can rest now."

Incredible! All three scientists had pulled out just as I was ready to come. Damn it! Why do men always do that? I fumed. They'd missed recording my Big O by three seconds. I was still in a state of shock when the nurses returned.

"I was on the verge of a super orgasm," I explained. "Go tell them I want to continue."

"I'm sorry," one of them said, "the room has to be used for our next study subject."

I was unwired, still tumescent, feeling it was a terrible loss for science. But they were kind enough to give me another room down the hall where I could finish having my orgasm and go into resolution. I continued my fantasy, visualizing all their elaborate instruments blowing out in a blue blaze of sparks as I came.

Later I learned why my technician lovers had short-circuited my second orgasm. They feared it was the onset of a heart attack! According to their graphs and charts, ecstasy was hazardous to my health. Scientific nonsense! I'd been having orgasms like that for years. My heart loved the exercise, and I always felt terrific afterward—deeply rested and at peace with the world.

The readout on my EEG was fascinating, but what did it all mean? Raymond explained to me the scientific concept of brain activity producing electrical discharges with different frequencies, classified as beta, alpha, theta, and delta. We spend most of our waking hours in *beta*, the realm of ordinary consciousness and rational thinking. Here the brain waves are more rapid, slowing down at each deeper level of the mind in the above order. *Alpha* is the creative realm. Many times a day, a person unconsciously enters alpha during moments of intuition, inspiration, or while having a daydream. There is also alpha sleep or REM (rapid eye movement) sleep, during which most remembered dreams occur. *Theta* is deep sleep with little or no dream activity—the level for trance and hypnotic states. I had heard of yoga masters who consciously go into theta with meditation. *Delta* is the deepest level, where voluntary muscle activity is suspended and coma occurs.

The Rutgers experiment made sense. The minute I threw the switch on my vibrator, my brain waves registered alpha, and they stayed there throughout the entire masturbation sequence except just before the medium orgasm and again before the Big O they missed recording. At those points, my brain waves dipped down into *theta*. I was using a deeper dimension of my mind for experiencing pleasure. My brain was having a quick, deep, restful sleep, while my body was moving, heart pumping, blood flowing, and muscles flexing all the way through orgasm. This had all taken place in a waking state.

The EEG data confirmed that masturbation was indeed a delightful form of meditation! Performed as a conscious ritual, masturbation created harmony between my body and mind, the same way meditation did. Erotic meditation was practical, natural, and now scientifically validated. It provided natural healing of stresses, changed dis-ease to ease through discharge of sexual energy, and provided a transcendental experience completely in harmony with nature. Best of all, it was fun.

I had always thought I had to sit cross-legged in full lotus within peaceful surroundings to meditate. Actually, all the time I was drawing and painting, I was in the alpha state of meditation. Having sex and doing sports were both active forms of meditation. Once while swimming, I clearly remembered getting a "second wind," which was definitely a meditative state. The long-distance runner was meditating, and so was the weight lifter pumping iron. I proclaimed myself a long-distance masturbator pumping pleasure!

With my new understanding, tantra sex suddenly became real to me instead of just a fancy word. Tantra is an ancient science that consciously utilizes sex energy. Its practitioners create pleasure, power, and control over their own spiritual growth through increased sexual activity. It is neither yoga nor religion, although it has influenced both. The prescribed sex rituals involve prolonged sexual activity with repeated orgasms.

The tantra books I had read were all based on heterosexuality, so I thought the rituals were only done with a partner of the opposite sex. In the earliest tantric text, I later learned, women were the teachers. The highest form of tantra was ritual groupsex. The way I analyzed it, sex rituals covered an entire spectrum. The basis for spiritual growth was self, and the basic ritual was masturbation. Next came partnersex with the woman guiding the man in harnessing his energy to extend the time frame, prolonging sexual activity with repeated orgasms. The next step was the threesome, which broke through the conditioning of hoarding sex for one person, an important step in learning to live harmoni-

ously with others. Spiritual growth through sex was sharing sexual energy without emotional attachments or possessiveness. Peace and harmony came through the *collective energy* of individuals in the group rituals. In my workshops, each woman had an orgasm as we combined our sexual energy in a guided masturbation ritual—it was my design for tantra groupsex.

I came to see that masturbation is a meditation on selflove *only* if I love myself and perform a conscious ritual, creating a sexual celebration. My childhood and marital masturbation focused on not getting caught. I had trained myself to come quickly while remaining silent. Masturbating with guilt, fear, or anger was conditioning that reinforced my sexual repression.

The chain I started the day I added the euphonious subtitle to my little book was complete. I realized that I had been practicing meditative sex for some time, using sex energy to bring my body, mind, and spirit into perfect alignment with orgasm—a cosmic moment of joy.

CHAPTER ELEVEN

Looking at Addictions

Sex and drugs go together because it isn't easy to have fun against a backdrop of two thousand years of religious denunciation of bodily pleasure. Unfortunately, some of us get hooked, and the drugs replace sex. The most important thing I have learned about confronting an addiction is not to make it a moral issue. Being drug addicted, love addicted, or food addicted doesn't make me a bad person. I simply have a social dis-ease, and I am only one among millions who suffer from the emotional plague of repression. I am trying to get away from pain into pleasure, wanting to get out of the prison of my personality into the freedom of my essence.

Drinking was the natural thing to do when I wanted to have fun. It all started off so innocently. I enjoyed having a couple of drinks to unwind and feel less sexually inhibited before making love. Because I drank periodically rather than daily, I had the illusion of control. It took more than a decade to see that I had become dependent upon alcohol. The woman takes a drink; the drink takes a drink; and then the drink takes the woman.

After hundreds of sick hangovers, periods of depression and guilt, it finally dawned on me that if I wanted to upgrade the quality of my life, I would have to stop drinking. Contrary to the popular image of the alcoholic having to lose everything before hitting bottom, I was able to get off the down elevator long before it reached the basement. I was thirty-two when I launched my self-healing process, and it was an exciting rebirth.

Living without alcohol gave me the opportunity to learn how to do everything all over again. I couldn't have done it alone. I had a national support group of other alcoholics who shared their experience, strength, and hope with me. They showed me that helping others to recover from alcoholism was the best way to help myself. In no time at all, I became part of the universe instead of the center of it. I stopped being an egomaniac with an inferiority complex. As I gained respect for myself, I could begin to extend that to others.

It took me several more years to see that I had another major dependency—love addiction. I was using love the same way I used alcohol, to avoid looking at myself. With each love affair, I had an unconscious contract that had a bottom line: my partner was to provide me with sex and security. The next phase of dependency was acting like I was independent. I became the strong one who was needed. But needing to be needed was the flip side of the same coin of dependency.

Finally I took time out to learn how to enjoy my own company. Giving myself permission to have happy, independent orgasms freed me from the constant pain of sexual dependency. I paid more attention to the relationship I was having with myself, and selfloving led to self-healing. I discovered that security came from within, not from walking off into all those sunsets. Being with a friend or a lover was finally based on choice, not loneliness or neediness.

After nine years of sobriety, I discovered marijuana. Immediately I knew that this magic herb was going to save the world. Here was a high without a hangover, and marijuana was a guaranteed aphrodisiac. It turned my whole body into an erogenous zone with heightened senses. Time was suspended. The old linear censor with its "thou shalt nots" was replaced by erotic images circling my consciousness that seemed to come from an ancient source where creativity, sexuality, and spirituality were all one. It was a nonverbal experience. I couldn't draw it or describe it with words. It just was.

Although my friends assured me that grass was not addictive, I managed to turn an erotic ritual into a daily habit. With my moderate use of one or two joints a day, it never occurred to me it was a problem. Although grass was not a violent or dangerous drug like alcohol, it had a downside. I found it caused a loss of energy. Little by little, my ambitions were fading into dreams. A sudden drop in blood sugar caused the uncontrollable munchies, and frequently saliva or vaginal secretions went dry. A loss of REM sleep made my dreams disappear. Also my short-term memory was impaired. While marijuana seemed to enhance my intuition, the creative process ultimately suffered from my inability to stay with the details or keep track of their sequence and significance. The woman smokes a joint; the joint smokes a joint; and then the joint smokes the woman.

Toward the end of the seventies, along came Sister Cocaine. For a year I did it occasionally because it was such a fashionable high. But once I scored my own, I was instantly seduced and addicted. It took me back to clear memories of my obsession with alcohol, only this time there was no illusion of control. I did coke until it was all gone, rationalizing that Freud probably did the same thing. In ten months I'd written a whole book. I ended up throwing out the manuscript because my drug-induced arrogance had destroyed my critical judgment. In just one year, cocaine brought me to my knees. Feelings of paranoia became so intense that I went back to my support group to regain the peace of mind I'd known when I was drug-free. I concluded that, for me, all recreational drugs exacted too high a price. I stopped getting high so I could get free.

Striving for pleasure was my health, but dependency on a mood-changing substance caused patterns of repetition and more dependency. Drugs separated me from my experience and blocked possibilities for growth. An addiction could either wipe me out, keep me stuck in one place, or, if I confronted it, become a path to self-knowledge. Each drug taught me different lessons. Alcohol showed me the depths of despair, marijuana gave me experiences with ecstasy, and cocaine taught me about the misuse of money and power. In order to stay off a drug, I needed to have a support system and be open-minded about living with spiritual principles. I didn't have to believe in a formal God, but I had to believe in some kind of power greater than myself that I defined. First the group was my higher power, and finally it became my higher self, the Goddess within.

After years of stopping and starting, I finally parted company with cigarettes, my constant companion of forty years. Maybe it was because I thought smoking cigarettes was my last addiction that made it such an emotional issue. I grew up thinking that a person who didn't smoke or drink was a religious fanatic or a prude, so every time I lit a cigarette, I felt marvelously human. No one could accuse me of being a purist, a health nut, or a square. The withdrawal symptoms from coming off cigarettes were far worse than those from any other drug. Long after the actual nicotine cravings had ceased, I still had to deal with all the insecure feelings that I had been hiding behind the smoke screen. If our legislators want to talk about the death penalty for drug dealers, they can start with the executives of tobacco companies.

But I needn't have worried about being "completely drug free." After I came off nicotine, I was still addicted to coffee, sugar, and salt. Refined sugar and salt are two more hard drugs. Whenever I have a sugar slip, I get a fast "up." But it only lasts a short while before the inevitable crash with the "sugar blues." And I still occasionally shoot up a bag of salty potato chips. Salt retains body liquids, and I wake up the next day with puffy eyes and stiff joints. I remind myself that being a sugar and salt junkie isn't a moral issue. I don't demand perfection, only progress.

Many of the dangerous drugs are legal and prescribed by doctors to help us sleep, relax, pep up, lose weight, or avoid pain. Doctors have become legitimized drug dealers. I have no personal experience with pill addiction, but it seems to me that tranquilizers, barbiturates, and Quaaludes are alcohol in pill form, and amphetamines are solid cocaine. Diet pills are the curse of womankind. Many of those slim, feminine bodies are housing devastated central nervous systems that cause mental and emotional confusion. Every day millions of people cross over the invisible line into an addiction by taking pills "according to doctor's orders." The woman takes a pill; the pill takes a pill; and then the pill takes the woman.

I spent the first thirty-five years of my life feeling like a dependent child running to doctors for answers they seldom had. I finally turned to natural healing and became my own doctor. Along with changing my diet, I began experimenting with fasting, enemas, colon irrigation, herbal remedies, and bathing rituals. Because there are so many different approaches to nutrition and healing, I apply the same rule I use for sex: There is no one "right way."

Meanwhile, my transition diet is based on offering myself delicious alternatives from Mother Nature's produce as I withdraw from man-made products. I'm principally a vegetarian. Phasing out animal and dairy products has eased my arthritis and I stopped getting the common cold. The hormones and antibiotics administered to livestock and poultry, plus the nitrates and nitrites used to preserve animal flesh are all harmful. Most degenerative diseases are not part of the natural aging process; they're caused by sedentary life-styles and the consumption of devitalized processed foods. Preservatives and additives are all addictive and most are carcinogenic. In cold weather, I use the macrobiotic diet of fish, cooked grains, steamed veggies, and green salads. I also consume lots of fruits, veggies, and leafy greens just the way they grow. Fresh herbs, lemon juice, cayenne pepper, dried vegetable seasoning, and fresh garlic spice up my salad bowl. Garlic is the "natural antibiotic." It purifies the blood and aids digestion.

Whenever I want a dramatic healing, I start juicing. A liquid diet gives the digestive system a rest as my body heals itself. I like the short, three-day fasts. Longer periods require important specific information about how to break the fast. Overeating is probably public-health enemy number one, and constipation gets second place. Fasting, enemas, and colon irrigation are all healing processes for both problems. Colon therapists are the cosmic plumbers of natural healing.

The laying on of hands is the best remedy I've found for coping with stress. I get a professional massage on a regular basis. I've had chiropractic adjustments, Swedish and Shiatsu massage, and Rolfing, which is deep work on the connective tissue. The combination of massage and sauna is far more effective than taking tranquilizers. I love all the bathing rituals of wet or dry heat, hot or cold tubs, sunbaths, mud packs, herbal wraps, and natural hot springs. They're all ancient healing techniques. The skin is the body's largest organ of elimination. Health clubs and spas are proliferating across the country as people are becoming more interested in exercise and good health—the ultimate aphrodisiac.

One afternoon in the steam room, a woman told me how lonely she was because her lover was on an extended business trip. Every night she went home to her empty apartment and tried to fill the void with food and television. She was gaining weight and feeling more depressed each day. I told her that although I lived alone, my busy schedule required that I set aside time to be with myself. An evening alone was very precious to me. I described some of my current selfloving rituals. She was so inspired she couldn't wait to get home to begin a love affair with herself. We can all heal ourselves with massive doses of selflove and orgasms by designing and practicing our own individual rituals of pleasure.

Being an addict affects my body, mind, and spirit. The healing process goes on each day as I continue to move toward a drug-free consciousness. Meanwhile I count my blessings. Thanks to selflove, I experience more pleasure in sex than I once did. I have better health through exercise and eating natural foods. Practicing various forms of meditation, I continue to improve my understanding of higher powers in the vast universe. This knowledge guides me in my daily choice of saying yes or no to my addictions.

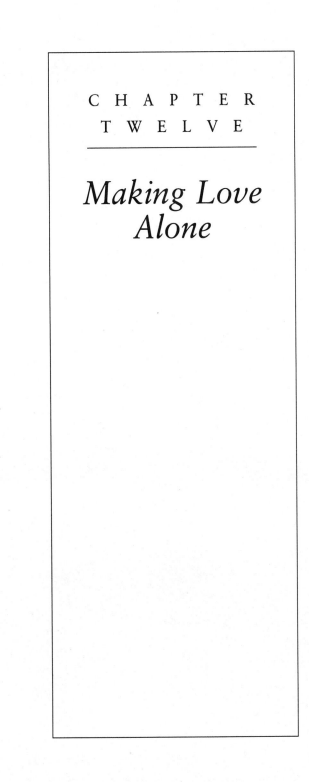

C H A P T E R
T W E L V E

Making Love Alone

Since most of us struggle with periods of self-hatred, bad body images, shame and confusion over sex and pleasure, I recommend having a hot love affair with yourself. Sexual healing begins by learning how to turn yourself on, discovering your sexual fantasies, and giving yourself an abundance of selflove and orgasms.

Let me take you step by step through a selfloving ritual that includes a sensuous bath, body appreciation, a selfmassage, genital exploration, and mirror dancing to practice the moves of sex. The ritual ends with an orgasm in the erotic setting of your design. You may want to move through all these steps or pick and choose among them to create your own variations, experimenting with different fantasies, vibrators, dildos, and other sex toys. Enjoy yourself.

Step 1: LOVING YOURSELF

Start the process now. Look into a mirror and say to yourself out loud, "I love you." Smile. Say "I love you," and add your name. It may seem strange, even make you feel embarrassed or foolish, but do it! Every time you catch yourself getting on your own case, stop and forgive yourself. Count your blessings. Give yourself a hug. Look into the mirror and say, "I love you just the way you are." If you do this simple exercise every day for two weeks, happy little miracles will start coming your way. Then you'll be inspired to do it for the joy it brings.

Step 2: THE SENSUOUS BATH

Taking a hot bath is a wonderful way to begin a selfloving session. The bathroom is often the only place that offers privacy from your family. It can be turned into a romantic hideaway simply be adding candlelight.

Have on hand your favorite scented soap, bubble bath, and coconut oil. Any kind of vegetable or nut oil in the water turns your tub into a hot oil bath. Try humming a tune, singing a song, or turning on your transistor radio. Sink into the hot water, and, with each breath, let go. Relax!

Touch your body tenderly all over. Review a memory of a sexual experience that was pleasurable. Think of an exciting scene in a movie. Tell yourself a sexy story, and try to include all the secret little things that cause a flutter in your stomach. Let your imagination go—no one but you is listening to your erotic tale. Your fantasy has no limits. As your thoughts warm up, let your fingers or your whole hand slide over your genitals; move up and down; feel the sensuousness of the slippery oily water on your clitoris or penis. Breathe. Experiment with going slow, then fast, soft, or firm. Be playful with yourself.

Step 3: BODY APPRECIATION

After you dry off, stand nude in front of a mirror in candlelight (not harsh electric light). Look at your image with compassion. Never mind the flaws—you know them all too well. Find things about your body to like and compliment yourself. If you were looking at a lover, you would praise the qualities you love. Give yourself that same kind of generosity. Forget comparisons. You are unique. If you are large, love your bigness. Be a gorgeous, Rubenesque nude, a sumo wrestler, a magnificent Amazon. If you are thin, love your smallness. Admire your wiry muscles and elegant angles. Appreciate your fleetness. Be a radiant nymph or faun. You are a divine work of art.

Step 4: DO-IT-YOURSELF MASSAGE

Doing selfmassage while sitting in front of a mirror is a lovely way to continue your selfloving session on dry land. It's an adventure in self-discovery. Lightly oiling your body, watch as you press and stroke yourself, first firmly, then softly, finding the sore spots that need rubbing and loving. Open your mouth as wide as possible, stick out your tongue, and open your eyes wide. Now scrunch up your face and tighten all the muscles. This releases a lot of facial and jaw tension.

Roll your head, breathing out loud, sighing, letting go. Press into the tight cords in your neck. Put your thumbs into the base of your skull, and then rub your head all over. Grab little handfuls of hair and tug. Rotate your shoulders forward and back, then press your fingers into all the muscles you can reach.

While massaging your breasts or chest, gently pinch and pull on your nipples. As they get firm, flutter your fingers over these little points of pleasure. Love your nipples. Tickle yourself with feathery touches on the side of your rib cage. Release your stomach muscles, and massage your whole stomach area with circular motions. Love your belly. Pat it and hold it with both hands. Now tighten the muscles, and pull your belly in. Let it out, pull it in, and let go.

Saving your genitals for last, move down your thighs, kneading the flesh and muscles like dough. Pull up one foot and oil it, carefully going between each toe. Press your knuckles into the soles of your feet. Pay attention to how each pressure point feels. It's the laying on of your own hands for self-healing.

Step 5: LOVING YOUR GENITALS

Women

For this step, you'll need a makeup mirror that stands by itself so both hands will be free. Any small mirror you can prop up against the wall will do. Find a comfortable sitting position where there is good lighting, perhaps under a lamp or near a window. If you like, you can use the magnifying side of the makeup mirror.

Explore your genitals with just as much interest as you have always examined your face. Pull your outer lips apart, smoothing away your pubic hair. Look inside your vaginal flower. Arrange your inner lips decoratively around your vaginal opening. There's a great deal of variety in female genitals, so your inner lips may be insignificant, small, large, or just medium, smooth or textured, symmetrical or one completely different from the other. All these variations are normal and beautiful. Which is yours? Do your inner lips attach at the base of your clitoris, or do they form an arch over the top of your clitoris?

Examine your clitoral hood, and follow the shaft of your clitoral body. Pull the hood back to expose the tip of your clitoris. Is it a different color? Does it look like a tiny seed pearl or a pointy pink jewel? Size or shape has nothing to do with how well your clitoris functions sexually. Love your clitoris! Touch it with your oily finger and explore the different sensations as you lightly caress the tip. If you can't see the tip of your clitoris, then put a finger on either side of your clitoral shaft and move back and forth, letting your fingers feel this little ridge of pleasure. Rub your clitoris a moment and see if it doesn't pop out a bit more with your tender touch. Look carefully to see if there is a change in the size and color.

Next, gently and slowly penetrate your vagina with your finger. Feel the ridges of the vaginal barrel. See if you can touch the tip of your uterus. With your finger still inside, take a deep breath and relax your hand, your arm, all your vaginal muscles, and your anus. Take another deep breath, inhaling all the way down to your pelvic floor, letting everything go. Spend a few peaceful moments being inside yourself, loving your vagina. Move your finger to twelve o'clock. Using a beckoning motion, observe the sensation. Don't concern yourself with finding a "G Spot"— just press around inside your vagina, noting the different feelings. Circling your finger gets vaginal juices flowing, making wet sounds and bubbling noises.

Now slowly withdraw your finger, and with an open mind, look at your vaginal lubricant. Is it clear or milky? Either one is okay. Does it taste salty, neutral, or a bit metallic? Does it have a hint of musk or an aroma like yeast in rising dough? Get to know how you look, taste, and smell, and how your vagina varies from day to day.

Sometimes the interior of a vagina can smell similar to a morning breath—a bit stale and sour. It's the natural process of cells breaking down and being discarded. Our bodies don't natu-rally smell like a rose. There are many different fragrances of sweat, lubricant, and sperm. Some people like an edge of raunch, a pungent odor. Others prefer a deodorized and perfumed body. Each of us is in charge of our own cleansing rituals and preferences for bodily odors. Just remember that eye butter, earwax, nosebugs, belly-button fuzz, cunt juice, jism, and dingleberries are all facts of a living body.

Men

Although it's easy for you to see your genitals when you hold them in your hand and look down, it's informative to get a frontal view. The magnifying side of a makeup mirror can give you a new perspective on what my dad used to call "the family jewels."

There's a great deal of variety in men's genitals, so your penis may be small, large, or in between. A small, flaccid pinkie can triple its size with erection ("the surprise package"). A very large dork usually doesn't grow much larger, but just gets hard. Most erect penises will be somewhere in the four-to-nine-inch range, but of course there are exceptions. Thinking one's penis isn't big enough is by far the most common worry among men. And it is a concern that can have a negative impact. If you have any sexual doubt based on genital size, clear your mind of this concern immediately. Remind yourself that many presidents, kings, and multimillionaires have been very small in stature. The old saying is really true: it ain't what you got; it's what you do with it!

Most Americans are guilty of being "size queens," including me. The first time I bought a dildo, I went for the huge twelve-incher, but I never used more than the first six inches. Eve's Garden, a sex boutique for women, just added a new dildo to its fall line because of the many requests for a shorter and fatter one. Now there is "Suzie Q" which measures 5½ inches by 1⅝ inches. The most popular size range of dildos sold to women is five to seven inches, which is probably the average cock size. While I believe genital size is relevant, and there is such a thing as the "right fit" between cocks and cunts, it's not everything. And remember that when it comes to sucking, an ideal form of stimulation for both men and women, smaller is certainly more manageable.

Now examine the head of your cock, the glans. If you're circumcised, your glans is totally exposed; if not, pull your foreskin back. Is the head of your cock small and pointy, a flat knob, or shaped like a mushroom with a flared edge? Size and shape has no relation to your pleasure, so love your cock no matter what style you are! Touch the tip with your oily fingers and explore the different sensations. Where's the most sensitive spot—on the underside, where your glans meets the shaft, or the whole rim around the head of your dick? Are your genitals dark brown or pink? Is the glans a bright red or lavender colored?

And what about your testicles? Touch your scrotal sack and feel the two little balls inside. Testicles and ovaries are equivalent glands. The male glands manufacture sperm to fertilize the eggs produced by the female glands. Extreme cold or heat effects sperm, so your scrotal sack regulates the temperature of the testicles by pulling them close to your body for warmth, or letting them hang long to cool. Gentle fondling or holding your balls while masturbating can be very pleasurable, I'm told.

Anal penetration with masturbation can also enhance orgasm. A friend of mine likes to masturbate kneeling over a dildo that stands on a base. As he strokes his cock, he slowly eases down on the dildo. When his body snaps with orgasm and ejaculation, he is sitting on the dildo with full penetration. He feels that anal penetration balances his yin/yang energies by putting him in touch with the divine female principle of opening and receiving. Many men have told me that the sensation is wonderful when their partner inserts a finger in their anus during oralsex and massages the prostate gland. This is something you can do for yourself during masturbation and it may open up new avenues of delight if you have never tried it before.

Step 6: MIRROR DANCING

Mirror dancing lets you practice the moves of sex. When you're alone, you can let it all hang out. Be free. Try any outrageous moves you can think of. Rotate your hips, do bumps and grinds, shimmy and shake. Wear a jeweled belt around your hips and make the moves of a belly dancer. Or pretend you're a priestess performing temple dances of erotic love. Or become a martial artist dancing with power, standing in the "horse posture" while using your vibrator. Masturbating in front of a mirror will give you an image of yourself as a sexual being. You might want to dress up in sexy lingerie or a fancy G-string and be a porn star masturbating for an imaginary audience. Be a mistress or master of the exquisite tortures of self-inflicted pleasure by adding a few interesting black leather items. Learn how to be your own sex object as your erotic personas emerge. It's all about having fun playing with yourself, getting off on the energy of your own sexual image.

Step 7: SETTING THE STAGE

If you decide to culminate your selfloving session in your bed-room, be sure you've made it the most erotic environment you can. How would you decorate or prepare your bedroom for a very special lover? That's the same thoughtfulness you want to give yourself. Lighting, color, sensuous fabrics, soft pillows, and music are basics for creating an erotic setting. You might put erotic art or photographs on your wall. Experiment with different candles, such as small votive lights in colored glasses, or perhaps tapers in candelabras. Candles will burn freely if you pour off the melted wax every few hours. The edges of large column candles can be shaped into petals when the wax is warm. (To remove spilled wax on rugs or fabrics, let it dry and then use a hot iron over paper towel, which soaks it up.) Other sources of soft lighting are a fireplace, or a small lamp with a low-watt colored

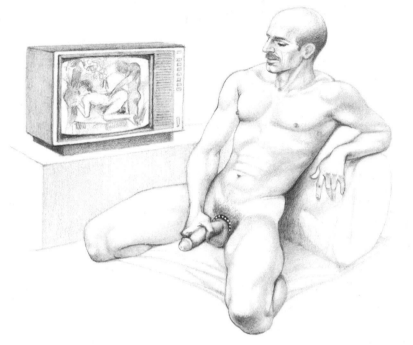

bulb. You can even use the changing light from a television screen with the sound turned off.

An erotic environment appeals to all your senses. Light incense or spray a bit of perfume on your pillow. You can arrange a pretty tray of sensuous fruit to put beside your bed—mango, kiwi, or papaya slices—along with a bubbling glass of champagne, ginger ale, or fruit juice in a pretty stemmed glass. If you prefer grass, have your rolled joint and roach clip ready on the tray. Be sure to take the phone off the hook, or turn on your answering machine with the volume down. Soft music is relaxing, and hard rock is exciting, or perhaps you prefer the sound of the surf or falling rain. With or without music, remember to listen to the sound of your breathing. Have your sex toys available. Maybe you want to have a fantasy while looking at sexy photographs or reading an erotic book. Perhaps you've brought home a new video porn tape.

Step 8: "LIGHTS, CAMERA, ACTION"

Now that the stage is set, get comfortable by stretching out and taking a few deep breaths. Say "I love you" in your sexiest voice. The scene calls for slow motion, so take your time and be a gentle lover for yourself. Run your hands over your body. Touch your nipples. Massage your genitals. Bring yourself up slowly. Don't think about orgasm—think about the good feelings as you play with your body and your fantasies. When you feel yourself getting close to coming, drop back by intensifying your breathing and tightening your ass muscles. Tease, squeeze, and please yourself. Try to spend at least thirty minutes.

When you finally soar into orgasm, let your joy be heard. Give yourself permission to sigh, to laugh, to moan, or utter any kind of sound that might bubble up. Just for fun, you might want to go on riding the waves of pleasure by continuing stimulation. Take yourself into another buildup with a second orgasm. Pleasure heals all those sexual inhibitions.

We want to remember that there will always be different strokes for different folks, at different times, at different places along the infinitely varied path of pleasure.

One Bodysex woman had her own version of a selfloving session. Her private time was during the day when her husband was at work and the kids were in school. She would stretch out on her couch in the living room fully clothed and use her vibrator for ten minutes. Then she would stop and go about her housework. After a while, she'd return to the couch for another ten-minute session of vibrating. After a couple of hours of "masturbation interruptus" she would have an intense orgasm that left her feeling marvelously refreshed.

An adventuresome friend of mine created her own version of S & M masturbation. She wore a slave collar and silver-studded black leather wrist cuffs. Then she applied a touch of mentho-

lated Tiger Balm on her clit and spanked herself with a leather
paddle to warm up her bottom. Once she was turned on, she put
tit clamps on her nipples and began vibrating while she fantasized an elaborate bondage scene in which she got tortured with
pleasure by a cruel, beautiful mistress.

Another more conservative friend liked romantic masturbation. She loved to read trashy romance novels. Her favorite
fantasy was imagining herself as a teenager on her first date. The
young man varied, but he was always handsome, sweet, and
completely inexperienced. They would kiss for hours until she
got so aroused that she finally talked him into going all the way.
Her scene always took place in a parked car in the moonlight
with a love song playing on the car radio.

Over the years, I've experimented with many different ways
to make love to myself. But that doesn't mean all of my selfloving
sessions are elaborate or exotic or filled with sexual fantasy.
There have been nights when I've vibrated in bed, watching
television, because I was in the mood for just a casual orgasm

before drifting off to sleep. Teaching masturbation in the Bodysex Groups has kept me interested in trying new things. Otherwise I might still be masturbating with my wedding-night fantasy.

Sometimes I'll start a selfloving session with a fantasy and find it's not working. Then I mentally flip through my current repertoire until I get one that's hot. If the fantasy ends before I've had my orgasm, I rewind the film and play it again until I come at the end of the reel. But sometimes I can't direct my mind into erotic scenarios. Then it's time for sensate focus—simply feeling my body. Without being judgmental, I observe the mental chatter in my head while I keep going back to the sensation in my clitoris. It's similar to repeating a mantra while meditating, losing it for a moment, and then remembering to return to it again. Dipping in and out of clitoral awareness will eventually quiet my mind so I can have an orgasm.

A sex toy can add variety to your selfloving and encourage experimentation. The best way to buy one is to see and handle it yourself, but sexshops aren't available to everyone, so the next best thing is browsing through a sex catalogue. But beware, many ads in national sex magazines sell shabby or misrepresented sex toys, taking advantage of the fact that most people will not complain. Two of my women friends own sexshops, and you can write for their catalogues and buy with confidence. Both carry sex books that might interest you. They are Eve's Garden (119 West Fifty-seventh Street, New York, New York 10019) and Good Vibrations (1210 Valencia Street, San Francisco, CA 94110). Another reliable company is the Xandria Collection (874 Dubuque Avenue, South San Francisco, CA 94080).

Vibrators come in a variety of sizes, colors, and styles. Battery-operated vibrators have the advantages of portability and gentle vibes, but the batteries don't last very long and can go dead at the most inconvenient times. Oster makes a rechargeable vibrator that's cordless with about an hour's worth of vibrating before it needs to be recharged. I've taken this one out on the sun deck and to the beach. There are a number of wand-type electric vibrators produced by well-known manufacturers, but, in

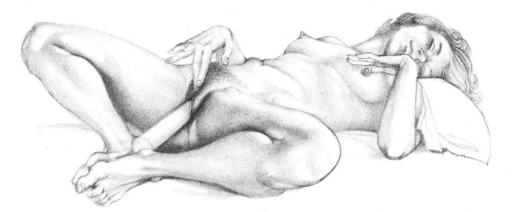

my opinion, none of them matches the performance of the Hitachi Magic Wand. It's well made, has a beautifully cushioned head, and doesn't heat up too much even after hours of use. It's interesting that the instruction manual says nothing about the sexual application of this quality massage machine, even though I suspect most people are buying them for sex. There's no danger of being shocked or electrocuted with a Magic Wand, even if you're vibrating a very juicy pussy. (Electric orgasms are absolutely safe as long as you keep the vibrator away from water.) The Panabrator by Panasonic is a powerful machine that's superb for massage. Except for a handful of sexual athletes, most women find its vibrations too strong for sex.

There are two kinds of light-weight vinyl caps that can be fitted over the head of the Magic Wand for vaginal or anal vibrating. One has a four-inch straight tip. The other one has a slightly curved tip and is called the "G-Spotter." Some men give the G-Spotter good reviews for massaging their prostates.

Butt plugs, which look like small dildos, come in a wide variety of sizes. They can be placed inside the anus by either men or women during masturbation to add an extra thrill. Any toy that's used for anal eroticism must be completely smooth and have a flared base so it doesn't slip all the way inside.

Vibrating the clitoris with vaginal penetration is combining the best of both worlds for some women. Silicone dildos are the most erotic because they're smooth and supple. Others are made of hard rubber or plastic, and they're often not visually appealing. Contrary to male fantasy, many women prefer medium or small-sized dildos.

Remember this rule for safesex: *Don't use a dildo in your anus and then go back inside your vagina.* It can cause an infection. It's safe, however, to go from your vagina to your anus. If you and another person are both playing with the same dildo, use two separate condoms or wash the dildo in hot soapy water before you transfer it from one to the other.

An organic dildo can be made from a cucumber or zucchini (I have a friend who's crazy about wilted carrots too). A cucumber can be sculpted to size with a potato parer, but leave enough skin on the bottom for a handle so your lover won't slip away in the night. If you carve too close to the center seeds, the cucumber will go limp. Cucumbers are naturally moist and slippery and have been used in beauty creams for years.

One day I was cruising the cucumber bin in a supermarket with such thoughtfulness that a woman standing nearby asked me how I knew which ones were best. I couldn't resist, "Mainly intuition," I said. "I'm picking out a lover for tonight." She doubled over with laughter as I winked and walked off.

Lubricants can be a useful aid for masturbation. Water-based ones are the safest and least likely to cause any irritations when used internally. Probe is an excellent water-based lubricant: it's odorless, tasteless, very slippery, and most resembles a woman's natural secretions. Some women prefer cold-pressed coconut, olive, apricot, or almond massage oils for sexual play. ("Cold-pressed" means the oil hasn't been heated or processed; it's in a natural state.) A few women find they can't use massage oil for a lubricant because it causes an irritation, however. Petroleum-based products such as Vaseline, cold cream, and mineral and baby oils are to be avoided as lubricants because they can build up on the mucous membranes. Also petroleum products disintegrate condoms and diaphragms. With a little experimentation, you'll find your preference for a sexual lubricant and sensuous massage oil.

There are many sexual novelties that are good for a one-night stand—vibrating dildos with special clit-ticklers, vibrating eggs on a string, and ben wa balls are only a few. Stories about the erotic potential of ben wa balls are greatly exaggerated. They're basically two metal or plastic balls that are worn inside the vagina—the theory being that the contact and movement will produce fantastic results. The best ones are called Duotone Balls, with the ball bearings inside hollow plastic balls about two inches in diameter and tied together with a string. When you shake your hips, you can hear them rattle. Pulling the Duotone balls out slowly while you're vibrating can be fun, but as for having "orgasm after orgasm" from just wearing them, forget it. If your fantasy about ben wa balls is strong, they may be good for a short-term thrill.

I never feel too disappointed with a sex toy that doesn't last, as long as I've had a little fun with it. Sometimes I go for months without using anything except my vibrator for masturbation. The best turn-on is still my fantasies.

Another sexual fantasy to come true was putting my weekend workshop onto a one-hour videotape. I was the producer, the writer, the director, and the star of the show. *SelfLoving,* video portrait of a women's sexuality seminar, is available through stores I've recommended on page 144. Or you can write to me directly to order my videotape. Send $45.00 (includes postage) to Betty Dodson, Box 1933 Murray Hill, New York, New York 10156.

The best sexual aid—one we often neglect—is a healthy, fit body. Depending on your age and physical condition, there are many ways to keep moving and using your body. Walking and stretching are two of the best exercises for anyone. People who engage in an active sport are fortunate because working out is a game that's fun. Dancing is a natural form of aerobics that can be social as well as enjoyable. Whether you dance socially or alone in your living room, your body will move within its natural limits because dancing isn't competitive; it's just pleasurable.

Yoga is also noncompetitive, and the postures are wonderful for stretching the spine, flexing the joints, and coordinating breathing with movement—all assets to sexual health. It's great that so many people are working out. I'm doing water aerobics in a pool four times a week and I love it.

Someday everyone will openly acknowledge sex as the original aerobic exercise. When we have happy, full-bodied orgasms, our breathing deepens, hearts beat faster, skin sweats, muscles flex. Our minds are at peace when we're going for the Big O.

Our society is so anti-sexual and anti-aging, that many of us give up on sex when we get older. But I'm happy to report that women in their sixties and seventies are showing up for my workshops to learn more about orgasms with selfloving.

The PC muscle (pubococcygeus) is responsible for the health of the pelvic floor in both women and men. A weak PC muscle can result in urinary incontinence, the seepage of urine during laughing or sneezing, a condition suffered by millions of older women. To locate your PC, simply stop the flow of urine by squeezing or lifting up on the muscle. Keeping this muscle toned will ensure urinary control, and consciously using it during sex will heighten the experience of orgasm, for women and men.

During my forties, I was aware of the delicious sensations that accompanied squeezing my PC muscle on my lover's penis. When we had a slow, rhythmic movement going, I would tighten my PC to heighten the voluptuous sensations. It was very erotic, a "suction fuck" instead of a "friction fuck." We lost track of who had the vagina or the penis as our genitals became one huge sex organ capable of repeated orgasms.

After I went through menopause, the lining of my vagina became very sensitive. Finger penetration without friction was okay, but even with lots of lubrication, the old in and out of penis/vagina sex caused an uncomfortable sensation and soreness. After careful consideration, I rejected hormone replacement. I wanted to age naturally. Maybe I'd go down in history as the first sexually active older woman who found happiness without vaginal penetration. Meanwhile, a full and active sexlife laid ahead of me with the pleasures of oralsex, analsex, phonesex, role-playing, sharing masturbation, and of course, all those wonderful orgasms I consistently had with myself.

Somewhere in my mid-fifties, I was at a party one night when I had a giant sneeze. Feeling a trickle of urine warming my panties, I inwardly groaned, "Oh no, now I'm gonna have to wear June Allison diapers." At first I blamed it on the aging process, and dipped into the doldrums of feeling helpless. After months of making constant references to "growing older," I finally began to challenge my beliefs about aging.

Urinary incontenance simply meant that my PC muscle was in a state of neglect. I went out and bought some small dildos, and I also got a vaginal barbell designed to work the PC muscle. Several times a week, I did fifty to a hundred repetitions to strengthen my muscle. Then I started putting my electric vibrator on my clitoris while I did my reps, ending the exercise with one or more orgasms. Surprise! Within several weeks, there was no more trickling of urine. I also discovered that as my PC muscle got toned, my orgasms got fuller. With a dildo or a barbell inside my vagina to work the muscle against, I started having those lovely "rock and roll orgasms" that I used to have with a partner who knew how to do a "suction fuck." With me doing the penetrating, it was as hot as any sex I'd ever had. Human sexuality constantly amazes me. Wonder what I'll be doing in my seventies?

Embracing my entire sexual life cycle and healing myself with positive images of growing older, I find that menopause has become my time of power with renewed self-confidence, strength, inner beauty, and sexual abundance. When I turned sixty, I began producing a one-hour videotape of the women's sexuality seminars I'd been doing for the past twenty years. After months of editing with my partner, Samantha, and constantly screaming

149

"Cut that," "Get me out of there," "We're on my orgasm too long," I finally surrendered my ego to art. There I was with my postmenopausal body, rounded belly, and gray hair, having a full-bodied orgasm for all the world to see. At that moment, I stepped outside the boundaries of my socialization and found myself at a deeper level of compassion. I had fallen in love with my older me.

Masturbation Stories

Over the years, I have received thousands and thousands of letters from people all over the world. In many I read about the writer's sexual suffering or sexual joy. Some were hesitant voices from slightly opened closets. Most were astonishingly frank and appreciative. On a difficult day when I would be feeling like a fool for wanting to liberate masturbation, I would open a letter and read about a woman who had just learned how to have an orgasm after reading my book. Or a man had written to tell me how much better sex was now that he and his wife felt free to masturbate. These letters always gave me encouragement, reassuring me that selfsexuality was an endless discovery of the universe and one's self. I think of them as love letters. They are powerful and poignant, always fascinating to read.

Many of the letters here illustrate points I've made in the book in slightly different forms. Some offer additional information from their author's life experiences. Others bring different perspectives and intriguing insights. All of the letters as they appear here have been abbreviated, and the names and places have been changed.

I love these intimate stories of protest, wonder, yearning, and joyful self-discovery; I love their reality.

Dear Betty:

I just experienced my first ever *guilt-free* orgasm masturbating. My method since I was four (I am nineteen now) consists of putting my arm between my legs and then humping and thrusting. I have now started opening my eyes and fully accepting the feelings my body gives me. It's so emotionally satisfying and strength building!

Blair C.
Westport, CN

Dear Betty,

I really don't know what it is exactly I want to say, so I'll start out with who I am. My name is Debbie and I'll be sixteen in about two weeks. My mom and I talk openly about sex, but never masturbation. It is I who become embarrassed. She bought your book *Liberating Masturbation* and she lent it to me last night. Although I have had sex quite a few times, I have never reached orgasm. I thought there was something wrong with me so I faked them. Last night, for the first time to my conscious knowledge, I masturbated after reading your book. The hand didn't work, so I tried a vibrator. I really enjoyed it, and I think I had an orgasm. I say think, because I'm not sure. I always expected some kind of wild headrush, and a time lapse of a few seconds of floating ecstatically on clouds the way girls did in "trashy" novels. As it was, it was as though my vaginal walls vibrated by themselves, or had convulsions or something. I was so happy I had gotten such pleasurable sensations. I just want to thank you so much for opening a new door of self-understanding.

Debbie
Scarsdale, NY

Dear Betty,

I am a thirty-two-year-old, married woman having a gay love affair which my husband doesn't know about. I wasn't coming in either relationship. Needless to say, I had a lot of inner anger going on and I desperately wanted to get in touch with my sexual self. After reading your book and then immediately going out to buy the Hitachi Magic Wand, my whole life has been changed forever.

I cry with delight just knowing I have the power in my own hands to please myself whenever I feel like it. What freedom, what an awakening! These pleasant waves/contractions are just beautiful. I feel like a small child learning about the delights of my body for the first time.

This past Sunday, my husband built me up to a wonderful orgasm without any time restraints, and it was wonderful. I ended this wonderful orgasm with a huge smile on my face!

Now I'd like to learn how to share the pleasure of a sexual dance with my female lover so we both may reap the benefits.

Zoe V.
Pomona, CA

Dear Betty Dodson,

When I read your article I truly appreciated your frankness. Just last week my gynecologist told me with embarrassment I might "involuntarily" play with myself at night to relieve sexual tension. She called it "a kind of masturbation." I was too embarrassed to explain that masturbation was very "voluntary." I want two copies of your book to liberate me *and my doctor.*

Violet B.

Baltimore, MD

Dear Betty,

Your book is an important contribution to the mental-health efforts of therapists. Last summer I worked with a middle-aged couple from Mexico. He was recovering from a serious illness which left him with a weak libido and a certain degree of impotence. His wife was still very much alive but could not seek satisfaction from outside sex. They were religious people who loved each other. They also were not willing to let their sexuality wither away. I introduced them to the idea of sharing masturbation and taught them how to use a vibrator. It was an exhilarating experience for me. I saw two people climb out of the blackness of depression and begin to laugh and play again. The "cunt positive" woman is a blessing to the relations between men and women. Thank you for your generous gift to society.

Joseph M.

Alexandria, VA

Dear Betty:

About three months ago I was a junior-high history teacher but I quit my job and have been spending the last few months trying to change my previously duller than dull life. I learned about your book through *Cosmopolitan.* Would you believe I even felt guilty at the time buying the magazine!

As a young girl I wanted to be a nun, so I never did anything about sex or enjoying my body. I felt it would downgrade me somehow. When I graduated from high school, I entered a convent and stayed for six years. I left because I felt like a hypocrite. There was no love in me to share with others.

Now that I know I can achieve orgasm (at least one way!) I feel so much more confident about myself, so much more interesting and alive. The simplest discovery about my body makes me happy. And discovering my body did for me what all that praying never did. It has made me more outgoing and able to live with others. I have a long way to go yet but I have confidence in myself now. I don't have so much fear and I'm looking forward to life so much more. I've also started doing yoga and love it. Now I hope I can take one of your workshops sometime.

Karen
Cincinnati, OH

Dear Sensual Sister,

After finishing your book this evening, I decided to have a "love-in" with my beautiful body in celebration of one of my favorite leisure-time activities, masturbation. I am "an old hand at masturbation," as it were.

In addition to some of the methods suggested in your book, I would like to list a few other pleasures of my own:

1. Temperature change. Cool hands or cool water on one's genitals is very nice.
2. Terry cloth against the genitals for a nice soft friction.
3. Masturbating to orgasm while douching, or giving yourself an enema opens the cavities and gives a nice cleansing feeling.
4. Masturbating with a partner in the bathtub and soaping one another's genitals while creating new pubic hairstyles with the soap lather is a lot of fun.
5. Masturbating in other environments . . . sitting on the toilet in Penny's Department store, telephone booths, etc. . . . add a refreshing sense of novelty (with a touch of "naughty").

I'm sure that these aren't all "Dana Originals." There are so many possibilities. Masturbation is one of life's most pleasurable activities and it's FREE!

Dana G.
Spokane, WA

Dear Betty,

I have been involved in masturbation for as long as I can remember. My earliest memories were around three years of age when I bathed alone. I had a bath toy rubber mouse that had a squeaker in it. I used to remove the squeaker from the mouse and fill it full of water. Then I would force the water out against my genitals ... HEAVENLY. At age four or five, I used to play "hospital" with the neighbor girls. We used to manipulate one anothers' genitals. I'm sure my mother would have had a heart attack had she known.

When I was seven one hot summer, my cousin and I stripped in my uncle's garage and participated in mutual masturbation, taking turns pouring water out of toy teapots over one another's genitals. I did all of this on the sly. My mom and dad were pretty religious, and I figured it had to be sinful.

I thought that I had made a brand-new discovery at thirteen, when I masturbated to orgasm for the first time. When I confided in a girlfriend over the phone, I told her very seriously about my discovery and that I intended to write a book on my invention when I grew up. I told her that I would probably make a million. Unfortunately, I was very disappointed to make yet another discovery by finding a detailed description of my invention in a sex manual while babysitting for the neighbors one night.

All through my early teen years I experimented with a number of "masturbation toys"—hairbrush handles (smuggled under my nightie to bed), drawer knobs (removed in the dark and replaced before morning), parts of my brother's toys, Vick's inhalers, douche-bag and enema-bag nozzles, and whatever else I could get hold of. I either "stuffed it" or rubbed it, whatever felt good.

When my mother bought a vibrator for her "tense shoulder muscles" ... (I'll bet!) ... I managed to plead "too much homework" on a few Wednesday night Prayer Meetings, so that I could have a little private sex orgy with her vibrator, and relieve a few tensions of my own. One night I set a record of forty orgasms in thirty minutes. From then until present, I have experimented with a number of masturbation methods, only in privacy however, when my lover is gone. She and I don't share quite the same philosophy on the subject, but we are working on it. So much for my history.

This is the first time I have explored my autobiography of masturbation, but I felt inspired to do so as an end to a beautiful evening of self love with your book.

Ginny J.
Phoenix, AZ

Dear Ms. Dodson,

I felt a need to write you because of the commonalities of your story and mine. I, too, am an artist and masturbation has played an important part in my life. I am a thirty-six-year-old divorcée with two young girls. When I was sixteen I had my first orgasm by petting with my husband-to-be. He became an engineer, and we moved to Texas. We had "perfect" clockwork sex à la marriage manuals, achieving simultaneous orgasm every time in a relationship of thirteen years. Also it became perfectly boring. Two weeks after my husband moved out of our apartment, I discovered my own sexuality—I who incidentally have an M.A. and thought myself enlightened.

With two small children I wasn't going to either prowl at night or stick my children by the pool while I slept with someone, as I saw my friends doing. Anyway, my desperate situation was money and a job. I couldn't even pay a sitter to go out. So I masturbated. This was when I discovered why I had felt so unsatisfied. I found I could achieve endless orgasms and always the second one, about five minutes after the first, was the deepest. It was a poetic, drunken, melting experience that scared the hell out of me at first—not only did my body open, but my mind and creativity also.

Now I am running my own gallery and am a "fighting rebel" determined to be creative and self-supporting, not be part of the stereotype factory world. As to men in my life, I've had a number of peak experiences since my divorce. They came about not through need for "tension release" but a desire for beauty, union, and closeness. You see, through masturbation, I have gained *freedom*.

Corrine M.
Austin, TX

Dear Betty Dodson:

I was so inspired when I read your work that I pulled the curtains on the window, let some of the bright afternoon sun in at the edges, and masturbated delightfully.

I clearly remember discovering my clitoris when I was nine, sitting on the john wiping myself. I discovered that if I wiped too hard I gave myself some kind of shock. I tried the trick a couple of times but then dismissed it as some quirk in nature, something that almost hurt, but felt good anyway.

I didn't do any more exploring until I was thirteen when I read my father's copy of the *Kinsey Report on Female Sexual Behavior* from cover to cover. I was fascinated that it was supposed to feel so good, and had to try out some of the ways of self-stimulation the book mentioned. Yes, it worked, but wasn't that good the first time. I concluded I needed practice.

Sometime later while looking through my brother's *Boy Scout Handbook,* I came upon the chapter that dealt with masturbation. There I learned the truth I had long suspected—it was not good for the development of my character. The chapter dismissed pimples and insanity but hinted that is was surely a nasty habit to be avoided.

By then, I was truly addicted to the sublime activity and felt the only drawback was the smell left on my fingers. So I found a old pair of white Sunday School gloves to use in my nightly pastime. I hid them deep in the bottom drawer of my chest but always feared the smell would give me away.

I was also sure I would somehow receive punishment later in life, that it would be impossible to have a normal orgasm with a man. Indeed, it went that way. My long list of lovers, I suspect, was just a quest to find a "come." I also felt I was reaping the just deserts of my childhood exploration of myself. I felt so guilt ridden that I couldn't bring myself to tell a man that I couldn't come unless he stimulated me directly with his hand. I was sure he'd guess I had been a masturbator. But mostly I was frustrated, angry.

After many years, I have finally accepted the fact that I need direct stimulation on my clitoris and that masturbation is the best kind of sex for me. I'm glad my compulsive "quest" is over. Your book is just great, the kind of support I've needed for a long time. I actually wanted to write a book on masturbation a few years back but found most women were too embarrassed to talk about it with me. Now you've said it all. Thanks for coming my way with your life and your honesty.

Patsy C.
Washington, DC

Dear Betty,

Until a few months ago, I had thought of myself as a sexual failure. My genitals were ugly and disgusting, my body all wrong, and my husband was very upset about my dwindling interest in sex.

I never masturbated consciously as a child or adult. Not

because I felt guilty about it, I just didn't know what it was. As a virgin I had one orgasm during petting and two orgasms with dreams. Other than that, nothing. Never during intercourse. Although I really enjoyed sex with my husband before marriage, I later lost interest as the excitement and newness wore off and frustration and failure set in.

Then two wonderful things happened. I showed my husband an ad for a vibrator and he secretly ordered one. When it arrived I opened it up and the first time I used it I had a orgasm! It was the most wonderful physical and emotional sensation. I loved it. One day I had eleven orgasms. The second thing was when I read your book. How close I feel to you and all other women who have had the same worries and concerns as me. Before reading your book, I thought orgasms with the vibrator were the first step, then manual masturbation to orgasm, and then orgasm with intercourse. I now realize how ridiculous and unnecessary these expectations are. I'm an orgasmic woman right now, fully functioning and able to take care of myself in one more important way.

Jennifer O.
Chicago, IL

Dear Betty,

There is so very much in your book that a nonmacho male can relate to. I find it quite incredible that at this stage in the so-called sexual revolution that the only works in praise of "self-pleasuring" are written by women—for women. When is a man going to be brave enough to write lovingly and intelligently about his masturbation in a way other heterosexual men can relate to? The myth seems to persist that masturbating is mostly a substitute for intercourse which for one reason or another is not available. Personally I can't imagine giving up masturbation even though I have a loving girlfriend. To me, masturbation is glorious fun for its own sake. At nearly sixty, I am today enjoying it more than ever. One aspect that rarely gets considered is that it is difficult to prolong fucking for a variety of reasons. Masturbation on the other hand can be prolonged ad infinitum because one is in complete control.

In your book you referred to the anguish you went through on discovering that your inner labia were of unequal length. Boy, do I identify with that experience! When I was a kid, I was certain that my exposed glans (I was circumcised but my younger brothers weren't) was the result of playing with myself. My mother's dire predictions had seemingly come true.

I don't think even you can imagine how much you and your book have done to help people everywhere to free themselves from hangups. Love from a grateful Canadian.

Perry D.

Toronto, Canada

Dear Betty,

Back in the mid-seventies, my lover and I of several years broke up. I discovered your book *Liberating Masturbation,* and it was very helpful and instructive. I liked that you cared about lesbians. I particularly enjoyed that you spoke with your mother about sexuality. At the time my mother and I were having difficulty talking to one another. I tried being open to her about my life-style, but somehow it just went over her head. She didn't want to know. She, too, is a unique woman, She divorced my father many years ago while in her early forties. To this day she has continued to be a sexual person, and she's now in her early sixties.

One evening she and I were having dinner and she was talking about her recent breakup with a lover of five years. I had just read your book and was feeling good about applying your instruction to my needs, so I decided to ask her about masturbation. We *never* talked about it in my youth—it never came up—which I thought was amazing. She got a little embarrassed and said she preferred sex with another person. But the conversation really became lively! She said, "Now that we're getting personal," and proceeded to ask me about my relationships with various women, my feelings about my life-style, etc. I asked her how she would feel, now that I was out to her, if I went public, how she would feel with family, friends, etc. It was a wonderful three-hour conversation, alive, warm, loving. And it totally changed our relationship—for the better!

Ellen A.
Philadelphia, PA

Dear Betty,

Since you are a feminist, you might object to this statement, but I do not believe that men should be taught they are the equals of women. Everyone would be a lot better off if all men were taught from infancy that they are, and always will be "little boys," and that they must always mind the girls. And, of course, the girls should be taught that it is their place to constantly supervise and discipline the boys regardless of age. I do not think it inappropriate for a woman to make a man strip, pose, march around naked, and masturbate.

Earl R.
San Mateo, CA

Betty, Dear Betty:

Finally getting around to telling you what a tremendously positive impact participating in one of your workshops has had upon my being! Initially it blew my mind, really stirred my inhibited innards. It was terrifying, yet beautifully exciting, and I survived, grew, and am still growing! Learning to love myself has been a fantastic experience.

I can never forget our last session, sixteen women all "plugged in" and "turned on," and you saying to me "stick with it!" How many times I've recalled your words and resisted the old impulses to pull away from that body surge, to withdraw, to quit. Stick with it I have!

For so long the words *sex* and *sin* loomed hand in hand in the recesses of my mind. Oh, sex was okay to fill my function of bearing children. But the notion that men might love me for my body and not my mind was a frightening prospect which I avoided like the plague. That is, until I learned to love me for my body and the pleasures it could give me. Now my loving mind and body have bridged that devastating gap and the union is beautiful. At first the trip across was terrifying. It took just one short month to span, a mind-boggling event at age thirty-six. Masturbate? Me? Yes, me!

Recently I found a new lover, and I astounded myself with my newfound boldness. I sprang my vibrator on him right away, and he loves it. Your name has become a household word. We love you.

Elly
South Orange, NJ

Dear Betty,

I have just turned twenty-nine. In a decade of being sexually active (over twenty different men) I have never had an orgasm, nor have I succeeded in masturbating to orgasm, ever. The nearest I came to coming was five years ago, using a bidet with a fountain. I got a vibrator last year but rarely bothered with it. I am like Nancy in your book who wanted to learn how but couldn't be bothered. I suffer from lack of libido (or suppressed libido, I should say). Erotic fantasies and literature turn me on, but again, I rarely bother. Now I've decided this is the year I learn to masturbate to orgasm! You may take much of the credit for instilling in me this ambition. Your joyful, unashamed outlook toward sex and masturbation is an inspiration.

I'm sure my sexual hangups and lack of desire stem from my

low self-esteem. This is another thing I have to change. I generally feel lethargic, ineffectual, helpless, and I know this is damaging. I'm going to see if a friend of mine who is a radical feminist and I can form a Bodysex Group like yours. All I know is sex should be enjoyed, and I am thoroughly fed up with missing out on the fun! I have to begin somewhere, and there's no time like the present. If you are ever in the U.K., please contact me. I want to give you a great big hug!

> Olivia A.
> Manchester, England

Dear Betty,

For over ten days I've been bubbling with joy. Never before in my life have I felt beautiful. Now for the first time since my partial hysterectomy, I feel beautiful—absolutely and positively beautiful—right from my head down to my toes, through my cunt. My genitals are actually pretty and not ugly as I've been told.

A woman in my social-science class noticed my joy and when I explained the reason, she said she was amazed, but delighted that I'd just found this old simple truth. She had always known that masturbation felt good so she continued to love herself even when her husband couldn't.

I am thirty-eight and she is thirty-three. When I showed her the genital illustrations in your book, the artist in her remarked how lovely we all looked. We then began to discuss how cold and unfriendly the world is to recently widowed or divorced women. In her house all the children need do is ask and immediately they receive a hug. She asked if I wanted a hug and I did. To our delight and surprise we sat and hugged for over two hours, nurturing our love-starved spirits. Such joy. It was all sparked by the clear, loving thoughts that had started while we discussed your book. Thank you for us both.

> Shirley C.
> Oakland, CA

Dear Betty Dodson,

I am twenty-three, have been married and divorced once and about to be married again. Since the age of eleven, I have been masturbating regularly and intend to continue until I'm too old to find my clit. Because you shared so much with me, I'd like to share a few of my experiences with you.

I've been a real bookworm since early childhood, so it's really no surprise that I got the idea of masturbating from reading the book *Candy*. I was lucky, my mother "caught me" once, and gave me a gentle talk about "those feelings" and "tension," and told me it was all right to "do it" to "feel relaxed." But she cautioned that doing it too often wasn't good for you. Of course, at this point, I was masturbating to orgasm two or three times a day, so when I tremulously asked her what was "too often," I was dismayed when she replied, "Not more often than once a week." However, even at my tender age, I reasoned that anything that felt so damn good and caused no apparent harm couldn't be all *that* terrible. After a brief attempt at "cutting down," I resigned myself to indulgence and devised several favorite methods, including using the jet of water in the bathtub, which I rationalized as "making sure I was very clean."

I was delighted to realize that many of the suggestions you mentioned were things that I had thought of, too, over the years. At fifteen, I discovered vibrators when I found one at home and became a regular with it. And a couple of years ago, I, too, started using a mirror to see myself masturbating. This idea sprang from a natural curiosity to see how I looked, getting aroused and having an orgasm, and there was no inhibition to stand in the way.

I often use masturbation to get in touch with myself. Sometimes at work when my eyes are bugging out from typing and I feel numb and stiff, I'll go into the women's bathroom, lock myself in the farthest stall, and masturbate quickly, reaching a sharp, intense orgasm in a minute or two. I find that this jolt to my nervous system makes me feel better and more productive.

Feelings about masturbating around another person, though, are a different story. But the man I am now living with is a warm, sexy, loving person (but young experience-wise), and he is anxious to learn. When he reads your book it's going to open a whole new door in our sexual relationship.

Pamela N.
Chicago, IL

Hello there, lovely lady,

I've lived with my old man Joe for six years now. He used to say to me that masturbation was a nice thing to do, that lots of women did it, etc. But I guess my conditioning was too strong. I was brought up knowing it was not a nice thing to do. I don't think I masturbated as a child, just explored my cunt and found I liked the smell. As I got older too many men were only interested in fucking so I never had my clitoris tampered with! Then I met Joe and he was gentle and patient. But I had this thing about my clitoris. I thought it was too sensitive to be touched. I assumed we were having such brilliant fucks who needed a clitoris?

After five and a half years the screwing deteriorated and we were starting to destroy each other. Then several months ago there was a big convention for feminists at the university. Three thousand women attended (huge number for here), including me. There were great evenings on feminist music, theater, poetry, etc., and many workshops, but the one that I was fascinated in was masturbation. Many confused women like myself listened to some really good ladies discuss their masturbation and techniques and orgasms. It was brilliant. Then came the answer to all would-be masturbators—buy a book called *Liberating Masturbation* by Betty Dodson. I really wondered if wanting to learn to masturbate warranted spending five dollars and what was the point lying in bed playing with yourself.

Back with Joe and our beautiful baby, I decided I'd better give the book a go! So I retreated to my studio and read the book, peeled a cucumber, got the mirror, the olive oil—you name it. Spent lots of time and nothing happened. But I enjoyed myself and had it firmly implanted in my head, "Don't expect orgasm the first time you masturbate." Well, the next week I read the book again, started on myself with none of the gear, and less than ten minutes later, I blew my head to bits with an ORGASM. I just smiled and said to myself, "Betty Dodson, you have changed my life!" For the next week, I was at it six times a day—I couldn't leave myself alone. I actually began to pulsate to the extent of discomfort at work. Halfway through something at work I'd go masturbate. I couldn't believe that I was experiencing such an incredible feeling. I knew that never before had I attained orgasm. The first thing I did when I broke through was ring Joe and tell him a fantastic thing had happened. We've never been better together—never! One part of your book applies directly to me, "Once I got free from thinking I had to get all my orgasms from fucking, it became pleasurable for the first time." Can you believe it—imagine being thirty before you find out what an orgasm is!!

Vicki T.
Auckland, New Zealand

Dear Betty,

About four years ago my marriage was on the rocks. My husband kept telling me I was frigid and should do something about it—namely masturbate. I couldn't remember masturbating as a child. I had tried only once as an adult, but it had terrified me to touch myself, and I stopped long before orgasm. In desperation, I spoke to someone on the staff of the National Sex Forum. He gave me a couple of paperbacks on sex and the only dildo he had left, a plastic one with batteries. I experimented with the dildo for a while but it seemed exhausting and hopeless. Then I acquired a big electric vibrator from a friend, and after several painful weeks learned to have an orgasm. I hated myself and was ashamed that I had to use a machine. I was sure no other woman in the world was so sexually maladjusted that she had to revert to such perversity for her gratification. I would often burst into tears when I finally had an orgasm. I felt I would never be able to enjoy sex with a man. I felt like a damned soul.

Then one day at the Museum of Erotic Art I saw a drawing of yours showing a woman masturbating with a vibrator. It was a big electric vibrator just like mine! I could hardly believe my eyes. I wanted to go up and touch the picture and examine every detail of that vibrator to make sure I wasn't seeing a mirage. A huge weight was suddenly lifted from my shoulders, and I've never forgotten you since.

After seeing your drawing, I felt less guilty, and pretty soon orgasms came easier. But I still thought the machine had ruined me. Then I fell in love with a man and soon I got the courage to talk to him. I told him about my clitoris, turned up the lights, showed it to him, masturbated in front of him and told him to hang in there with me, and lo and behold, it began to happen. I started having orgasms. Sometimes after he left and I hadn't had all I wanted I would get out the trusty electric vibrator and have another orgasm. I still don't have the courage to bring out my horse machine in front of my lovers, but I do have the luxury of wonderful feelings I thought would never be mine. So I thank you, Betty, for making that picture, and then for writing it all down in a book. It was bold of you and I appreciate it.

Anna L.
San Francisco, CA

Dear Betty,

I am thirty-seven years old and adore masturbation, always have. For about two years I've had a beautiful lover fourteen years younger than myself. Although he's the best I've ever had, only once did I have an orgasm with him inside. This was at a most unexpected time—I was feeling terrible about myself, i.e., fat, ugly, etc. He was terribly accepting, we made love, and I had an orgasm.

Why did it happen once? Usually when a man is inside me, I

feel very little and also how can his penis stimulate my clitoris if he is inside?

For many months I've gone back and forth on this question, sometimes accepting that that's how it is with me, and other times getting hung up on the "you're no good" syndrome. I think it would make a great difference to my peace of mind and self-esteem if I could figure this out.

Penelope K.
Montreal, Canada

Dear Sister,

In my second quarter of medical school, we were given a ten-lecture introduction to sexuality, which included explicit films of women masturbating in a laboratory setting, where researchers were investigating the physiology of the female sexual response. That was the first time anyone had told me it often takes a woman forty-five minutes to reach orgasm.

That was about five months ago. At the age of twenty-two, I had run through a motley collection of lovers, ranging from a truck driver to a yoga teacher, and I had never had an orgasm. I knew I was frigid, but after the film I started experimenting with my body and discovered that I could bring myself to wonderful orgasms if I took a lot of time (sometimes an hour). The first night I masturbated to orgasm I wasn't fantasizing—who needs fantasy? All I could think of was I FEEL. The sensation was its own trip. When I got more proficient, I added fantasy and found that it not only increased those wonderful sensations but also speeded up the process some. How great that I'll never need to fake another orgasm. It's really a shame that it's so easy to fake orgasm. Women get by with it because men are so undiscerning.

Right now I feel like giving your book to all my women friends for Christmas.

Ruth L.
Pasadena, CA

Dear Betty,

I have masturbated irregularly, sometimes with a lapse of several years, since the age of six, always feeling very sinful about it until about two months ago when I purchased *Our Bodies, Ourselves* and your book, *Liberating Masturbation*. Now I know that masturbation is normal and permissible.

I am forty-two years old and a virgin. I have never married. I agree with you wholeheartedly that masturbation makes a person happier and gives her a feeling of self-acceptance. This is the attitude that I have just developed within the past two months, since I finally stopped confessing my masturbation to God as a sin.

I am an only child. My parents raised me in a very strict, puritanical fashion and still tell me what to do even though they live five hundred miles away. I am a born-again Christian, and that is why it has been so hard for me to accept any sexual expression on my part.

Dolores S.
Richmond, VA

Dear Betty

I am thirty-three, female, married, and the mother of four small children, have a B.S. in chemistry and completed three years of medical school. I've masturbated since I was very young. Vaguely remember being discovered by my mother, receiving a long lecture, and, being a romantically devout Catholic child, guiltily confessing my mortal sin again and again.

I had a half-dozen affairs before I got married, but never experienced an orgasm during intercourse—in fact, have managed it only once without self-stimulation in twelve years. Got my first vibrator, a Christmas present from my husband, four years ago and enjoy it, despite the sometimes distracting noise. We have no electricity, so am restricted to battery-operated types. My husband, who has a strong libido, was becoming quite frustrated at my inability to climax, despite all sorts of acrobatics and innumerable positions. We finally came to the conclusion that penile stimulation just wasn't sufficient. After some experimentation, we found several positions that allow me to masturbate manually or with a vibrator during intercourse. The result has been an intensely satisfying sexual relationship for both of us.

Have you had any experience of masturbation as an analgesic? On a number of occasions, I have experienced moderately severe toothaches and found quite by accident that masturbating temporarily relieved the pain. Since I can manage multiple orgasms—five to ten is not unusual—I would just keep masturbating until a couple of aspirin took effect. I haven't figured out the mechanism of this, but it might be an interesting area of research. No, I haven't gotten up the nerve to mention it to my dentist.

Thanks for bringing this important subject out of the closet.

Lorna K.

New Brunswick, Canada

Dear Betty,

I bought your book because it was on a list of recommended readings for a Human Sexual Behavior course I'm taking at the university, where I am a senior in sociology. I've never before felt as bubblingly happy after reading a book. What a wonderful feeling to know my body is beautiful and not that smelly thing that men dislike but love to use. I will read your book whenever I start to feel "cunt negative."

Please send me another copy for my mother, who is sixty-three and still regards her body as foul-smelling like I did. She must have a dozen cans of spray. I'm going to get her a vibrator, too. I'm twenty and still living with her. I'm sure she'll be shocked at first, but it's a chance I'm going to take because I want her to feel as good as I do now.

Marie A.

Boca Raton, FL

173

Dear Betty,

Last night I read your book again and was just as fascinated as the first time. Afterwards I looked in the mirror and told myself that I loved me. Which was difficult at first. Then I lay in the bathtub and began caressing myself, saying "I love you, Donald" over and over. With one hand on my nipples and the other massaging my genitals, I kissed myself wherever I could, and shortly I orgasmed like I never have before. I ended up hugging myself while looking in the mirror with love, kindness, and understanding for myself that I never had before. It was difficult for me to get enough courage up to really love me and admit to myself that I am very sensitive.

Donald C.
Valley Stream, NY

Dear Betty,

Of anyone I've ever known, you will be the most able to appreciate this little autobiographical snippet. I used to have a fantasy partner way out in Denver whom I never got to meet. She's thirty-five now, single, and lives with a lover. We became partners in a wonderful way. One of my shirt-sleeve nephews found this girl in a Denver disco and must have played up my minor fame to her. He also mentioned that I was very lonely. She promptly sent me a letter, the first of fifty-nine (count 'em!), along with a picture of herself masturbating. Our letters, which spanned half a decade, were passionate descriptions of our sexual fantasies. Last year her lover became jealous, and she stopped writing.

Those were good years, I must confess. At ninety-one, all my parts are worn, weak, and powerless except my imagination. I miss her dearly.

Charles P.
New York, NY

Dear Betty,

I felt moved by your book to tell you my secret masturbation technique. I've been doing this since I was a teenage boy and I'm now thirty-eight. I masturbate with women's magazines. I apply dusting powder all over my erect cock, open the pages to the fashion or beauty section with pictures of women either clothed elegantly or in lingerie. I place my powdered shaft in the magazine and close it. Using both hands, I stroke until I have a beautiful orgasm. I hope you don't think I'm strange or weird.

I use all the different women's magazines—*Vogue, Cosmo, Glamour, Mademoiselle, Bazaar, Ladies' Home Journal, McCalls,* and *Seventeen.* Every month, it's like getting a new batch of lovers. They sure make my love muscle big!

I can make it with women of all ages—teenagers in *Seventeen,* coeds in *Glamour* and *Mademoiselle,* and middle-aged women in *Redbook.* I wrote to one of the editors to tell her what I did, and she wrote back, "Good for you! You're getting more out of the magazine than the girls are."

I didn't think about it when it first started, but these days it is also a surefire way of avoiding a disease.

Larry S.
Poughkeepsie, NY

Dear Betty,

Your honesty about your own sex life has inspired me to share a bit of mine with you. Twenty years ago, I had an office romance—the lady was a member of my car pool, and I had a private parking garage in the backyard of a house near the subway, which we took for the last few miles into the city. C's marriage was as sexually dull as my own, and we eventually got our act together by masturbating with each other at least one morning a week in the garage for nearly five years! It was probably the most exciting and satisfying sex I've experienced in my entire sixty-six years of life. C never wore panties—just a crotchless girdle and I would put on a rubber after showering those mornings I knew there would only be the two of us. We

175

usually reached simultaneous orgasms in about seven or eight minutes—what with some withholding on my part.

Those rare occasions like an office picnic or Xmas party when we got to actually fuck, it took me a long time and I don't think C ever did come. She used to say afterwards she preferred what we did in the car. There was certainly no doubt that she came quickly, easily, and intensely then. We made no secret from each other of our solo masturbation fantasies, which made the mutual masturbation even more heated. C said she never came with her husband and always finished herself off with her fingers while he rushed to the bathroom to wash off. How sad—but at least we found each other. When she moved to Atlanta, it took me a while to get over it. Well, nothing is forever. I did have a few other adventures, but none to compare with this.

Paul D.
Peekskill, NY

Dear Betty Dodson,

Your book has been read by the members of my professional staff, and we all agree that it will significantly contribute to the reduction of child abuse/neglect by teaching both males and females how to love themselves and in turn love their mates and children. With the exception of one patient over the last four years, nonacceptance of self-love has been one of the most common characteristics of male and female child abuser/neglecters.

W.T.E.
Del Mar, CA

Dear Betty,

After the workshop, I wanted to practice some of the things you suggested, but my problem is finding privacy. I tried shutting the bedroom door and telling my four kids not to come in without knocking, but they always forgot. I knew I had to find some solution, because learning to have an orgasm would make me a happier person. Finally, I installed a lock on my bedroom door and made a sign that read "MEDITATING—DO NOT DISTURB." I explained to the kids that I wanted my quiet time, and they were not to knock on the door unless one of them was bleeding. It worked!

Ruth V.
Scarsdale, NY

Dear Betty,

Frankly, I've been masturbating for many years and enjoyed every orgasm! I think masturbation is probably the most perfect form of sex. No worry about AIDS or any other VD. You can't get pregnant or get anyone else pregnant. And it's always there for you! You don't have to put up with the moods or whims of a partner. One woman told me that she can masturbate anywhere and even have an orgasm without anyone knowing—like on a bus or train or plane. She would just exercise her "Love Muscle!" (I can't remember the scientific name for it much less pronounce it.)

I enjoy using a vibrator too! I have one with a rubber cup on the end. When I am alone and feel the need, I put a sexy erotic tape on my VCR and turn on the vibrator with the rubber cup on the tip of my cock. It's a beautiful feeling when watching beautiful people loving one another (and sometimes themselves, which is a real turn-on for me). I may enjoy this for about an hour or more. Then when a good hot scene comes on and I reach the point of no return, I'll have a most delightful screaming orgasm! I don't always do this alone. Once in a while, I find a female companion who enjoys watching me while she masturbates, too.

Allan L.
Jacksonville, FL

Dear Betty,

I have to tell you about a contest I once had with a lady friend. Though it was about fifteen years ago, I still remember it vividly. We had a contest to see which of us could, using a vibrator, have the most orgasms in a three-hour period. Well, to make a long story short, she had seventeen orgasms, and each one was beautiful to watch! A woman is never more beautiful than when she is having an orgasm. And me? Well, I only had two! I tried for three but couldn't make it. What can I say? Only that since then I've known which sex is the superior one! I humbly bow down to women—but while I'm down there, maybe I can get in a lick or two and thus indulge in my main hobby, cunnilingus!

Stewart M.
Santa Fe, NM

Betty,

I'm sending a m.o. instead of a check because I'm a college student and my parents scrutinize my checkbook. I wouldn't want them to know I'm reading about the "forbidden sin."

I know you've heard everything but here's one: My aunt was hospitalized for excessive uterine bleeding. Before it was diagnosed as a fibroid my mom said, "See what happens when people play with themselves!" I said, "How do you know she did?" She answered, "I don't, but look what can happen (!!)" P.S. She's only forty-two and these are the eighties, can you believe it?!!

We're supposed to castrate ourselves (no premarital sex, no masturbation, no touching with a guy until you've been going out for a year). What do they expect anyway?

I've come a long way, though. My boyfriend and I can masturbate to orgasm in front of each other, and I found out that other friends masturbate, too. The guilt is diminishing.

Since I live with my parents, please send the book in a plain wrapping—I'm sure you understand.

Monica P.
Austin, TX